The Secret Seer's Arcanum
Presents
how
to Master the
Guitar Fretboard

A Simple Living Lens
for Thee to SEE and Learn
the Guitar Fretboard

/gē - Tahr/, /gi - taar/, noun.

   A medium sized, fretted, six-stringed musical instrument, where the strings can either be strummed or plucked with the fingers, or also struck using a plectrum in a similar manner.

Etymology: ancient Sanskrit (likely Persian influenced)

Literal translation: गीत (Geet) song, तार (Taar) wire/string
                   गीततार (Geetaarah) song wires/strings
                   गिटार (Modern phonetic adaptation; Hindi)

Copyright © 2025, 2026

Written and Published by Majestic Muse, United States of America. All rights reserved. No portion of this book may be reproduced, stored or transmitted in any form or by any means without written permission by the author or his heirs.

ISBN 979-8-234-00118-4

Re-Vision 0326-017

This work is presented as an artistic and exploratory expression. Musical theory and concepts are presented exclusively from a guitarist's perspective, and intended only for other guitarists. Some images may have been edited or manipulated to prevent any potential copyright claims. References, quotations, images, and ideas are included for symbolic, historical, and interpretive purposes only and do not imply endorsement. Meaning and significance arise through individual perception. The author assumes no responsibility for interpretation or application. Readers are encouraged to engage with discernment.

To the Player Who Enters

The path that begins here
is not for everyone.
But it will call to...

The hearts that beat pure and the minds that shine bright,
To the ones who still listen for truth in the night.
To those who take kinship of wood, wire, and tone,
And give each note as tribute to the Source alone.

Take these shapes as seeds, ever hold them up high;
Behold their geometries, born of the Clear Light.
Follow the octaves upon the ladder of frets,
Watch hidden patterns shine where darkness once set.

Throughout the field, hidden Eyes do watch the way,
Unspoken, unseen, yet present as you play.
'Tis time to take this key, and enter the lore,
Within, find the music; so above, be the door!

Learning the Fretboard
Step by Step

Introduction ...1
The Magic of Octaves ...2
The Unique Tuning of the Guitar ...05
42 Natural Notes in 12 Frets ...06
What are Chords & Triads ...07
Introducing the Cardinal Triads ...09
Review & Quiz ...14
Expanding the Triad Shapes ...17
Making the (m)inor Triads ...22
Augmented Triads ...24
Diminished Triads ...30
Dominant 7th Chords ...33
Basic Chord Formulas ...35
Afterthoughts ...36
Circle of Fifths ...39
Glossary ...40

"Don't only practice your art, but force your way into its secrets; art deserves that. For it and knowledge can raise man to the divine."
— Ludwig van Beethoven, July 17, 1812

Introduction

 At the time of this writing, I've been a guitar player for roughly 45 years. For much of that time, I wandered aimlessly, piddling around on the fretboard with very little understanding of it. I felt stuck in a deep rut, unable to find my way out. Then one day, it all changed. I stumbled upon something very interesting. *It* finally came to me. What I saw was a whole new way to *look at* the fretboard, different from anything else that I had seen before. It was then that I was finally able to climb out of my rut, and my skills were, at last, elevated to the next level.

 This book is here to *show you how to LOOK at and SEE* the fretboard. It all begins with a very special pattern of only three shapes (triads) from which everything else is derived. They are the divine trinity, the foundation upon which all else is built, and the point of reference to which everything returns. Learn these three shapes and their patterns. Learn how they extend up the fretboard and across the strings. Once you do, you can add to them, expand them, modify them, or mold them into any musical idea you like. This is the information that I wish someone had shared with me so long ago.

 Once these shapes are internalized, they will become second nature to you, and your hands will return to them without thought or effort. I now move freely and fluently all over the fretboard, up into the higher octaves, blending in different voicings and colors, in any way that I choose. The method shown here is simple, logical and systematic. But just like anything else worthwhile, it does require some study and practice. Some memorization and repetition is vital in the very beginning. But if you keep with it, following each and every step in this book, good results will be sure to follow.

 Although the method itself is quite simple, I don't recommend it for the absolute beginner. It's best suited for intermediate to early-advanced players who already possess a working technique and a basic understanding of music theory. I do not provide here any instruction on how to physically handle the instrument. That portion of the journey remains yours alone. Please understand: **What I am offering you here is not a comprehensive method, but a rather unique starting point —a LENS through which the fretboard can finally be seen** for what it truly is. From this perspective, you will be able to see it, navigate it, reshape it, expand it, and ultimately master it.

 Now, without any further ado, let us begin...

The Magic of Octaves

Just a Musical Theory?

Bear with me for the next few pages, because we're backing all the way up — all the way to the very beginning, to the most fundamental question: What is sound? For now, let us define it simply as energy vibrating through a medium (usually air), finding its way to the ear, transferring that vibration to the eardrum, and being interpreted by the mind as sound.

So, let's make some sound. Imagine striking a drum once per second. That is one vibration per second — 1 Hz. Now double it, and keep doubling it ...eight times in total: $1 \times 2 \times 2 \times 2 \times 2 \times 2 \times 2 \times 2 \times 2 = 256$. We arrive at 256 vibrations per second: 256 Hz. Each doubling of frequency carries us upward by one octave — eight doublings, eight octaves. And 256 Hz just happens to be the frequency of Middle C (Scientific Tuning). So if you could strike this tabla drum 256 times per second, you would literally be creating a Middle C note on the drum itself. Pretty cool, eh? But this is only the beginning — stay with me, there's so much more...

When you play Middle C on your guitar, the string is vibrating back and forth 256 times per second. Double that frequency to 512 Hz, and the note ascends one octave higher to the next C. Double it again — $512 \times 2 = 1024$ Hz, and it climbs yet another octave. Each doubling of the frequency lifts the same tone into its next harmonic echo: the same note, reborn on a higher rung of the ladder.

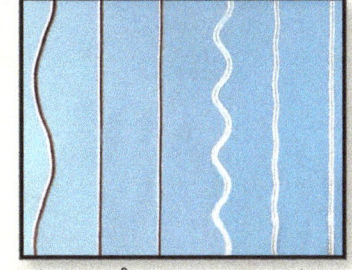

A photo of oscillating strings, taken from inside of the guitar sound hole.

But why is it called an "octave" if the frequency simply doubles? Because, in short, the average musical scale is created from eight notes (the diatonic scale). To see this clearly, let's look at the example below: this scale is in the key of Am, using the so-called 'modern' concert pitch tuning of A = 440 Hz.

Frequency	440	~494	~523	~587	~659	~698	~784	880
Note	A	B	C	D	E	F	G	A
Scale Degree	1	2	3	4	5	6	7	8

The eighth note is a repeat of the first note, but the frequency (Hz) has doubled. So if the first A is 440Hz, then the 2nd A will be double that at 880 Hz.

Below shows another example in the key of C, using the tuning of C=256 Hz...

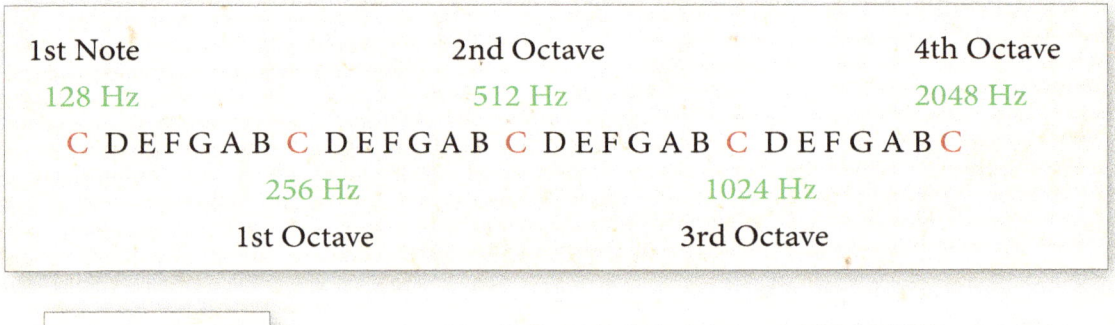

| 128 X 2 = 256 |
| 256 X 2 = 512 |
| 512 X 2 = 1024 |
| 1024 X 2 = 2048 |

Notice how the frequency of the C note doubles when it reaches the next octave

Play a C note on your guitar, then play another C note, either one octave higher or lower. Although you can hear that one note is higher than the other, you'll notice that they also sound like the same note. But have you ever wondered *exactly why* octaves sound so harmonious together?

The sine waves of a perfect 8th interval (octave)

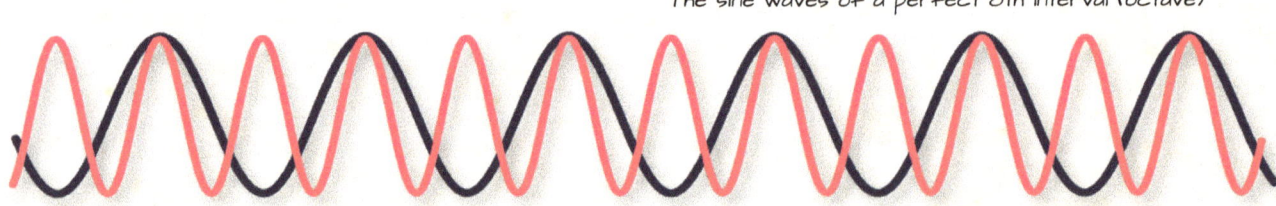

In the illustration above, the black wave is the lower C and the red wave is its octave. An octave has a 2:1 vibration ratio. This means that the higher note completes exactly two full wave cycles for every single cycle of the lower note. This creates a most simple periodic motion that our ears hear as pure consonance. To contrast the octave with a different interval, a perfect 5th, for example, follows a 3:2 ratio—the higher note vibrates three times while the lower vibrates twice before the crests coincide —so their crests coincide less often. In general, the more regularly the crests coincide, the more harmonious and pleasing the interval sounds. This is why the octave interval sounds the *most* harmonious.

But when we look more closely at the octave on the fretboard, we don't find eight frets— we find twelve. This is because an octave is divided into twelve distinct pitches when we include all the sharps and flats; this complete set of twelve notes is called the chromatic scale. The familiar eight-note scale (the diatonic scale) is simply a selection from those twelve—a chosen pattern of intervals long recognized for its natural beauty, balance and harmony.

As you move up and across the fretboard, you pass through the higher octaves. A guitar spans roughly three to four octaves, depending on the instrument and the note you begin with. These octaves repeat in a rising pattern, climbing higher and higher until the fretboard ends. Yet in truth, the *pattern itself* does not end there. The sequence of octaves continues upward—on and on, far beyond the limits of human perception. And just for fun, let's follow that idea a little farther…

Now imagine the fretboard stretching on without end. Begin with a middle C, and climb higher—octave after octave, until you've risen more than forty octaves above where you began. At that height, vibration has left the realm of hearing and entered the realm of sight; the frequency that once sounded like the key of C, now shimmers as green light in the visible spectrum.

This illustrates a deeper truth: sound and color are expressions of the same phenomenon—vibration—unfolding across different octaves. We perceive these ranges with different sense organs—lower octaves with the ears and the higher octaves with the eyes! Are you beginning to "real-eyes" the magic yet?

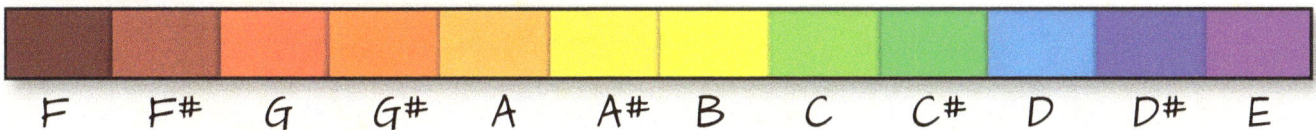

The visible spectrum of light sits roughly 40 octaves above the audible spectrum of sound. The illustration above maps the most probable corresponding colors for each note of the chromatic scale.

Image from the Flammarion wood engraving, artist unknown. I modified it, adding in the musical notes, hoping you might get the idea.

That which is above is from that which is below,
and that which is below is from that which is above.
— The Emerald Tablet

The Unique Tuning of the Guitar
A Ménage à Trois on the 2nd, 3rd and 4th Strings.

Moving from the bass E string towards the high E string, the guitar is tuned in 4ths, with one exception... a shift takes place between the G and B string. That interval is a 3rd. This tuning is unique to the guitar only.

See the following illustration:

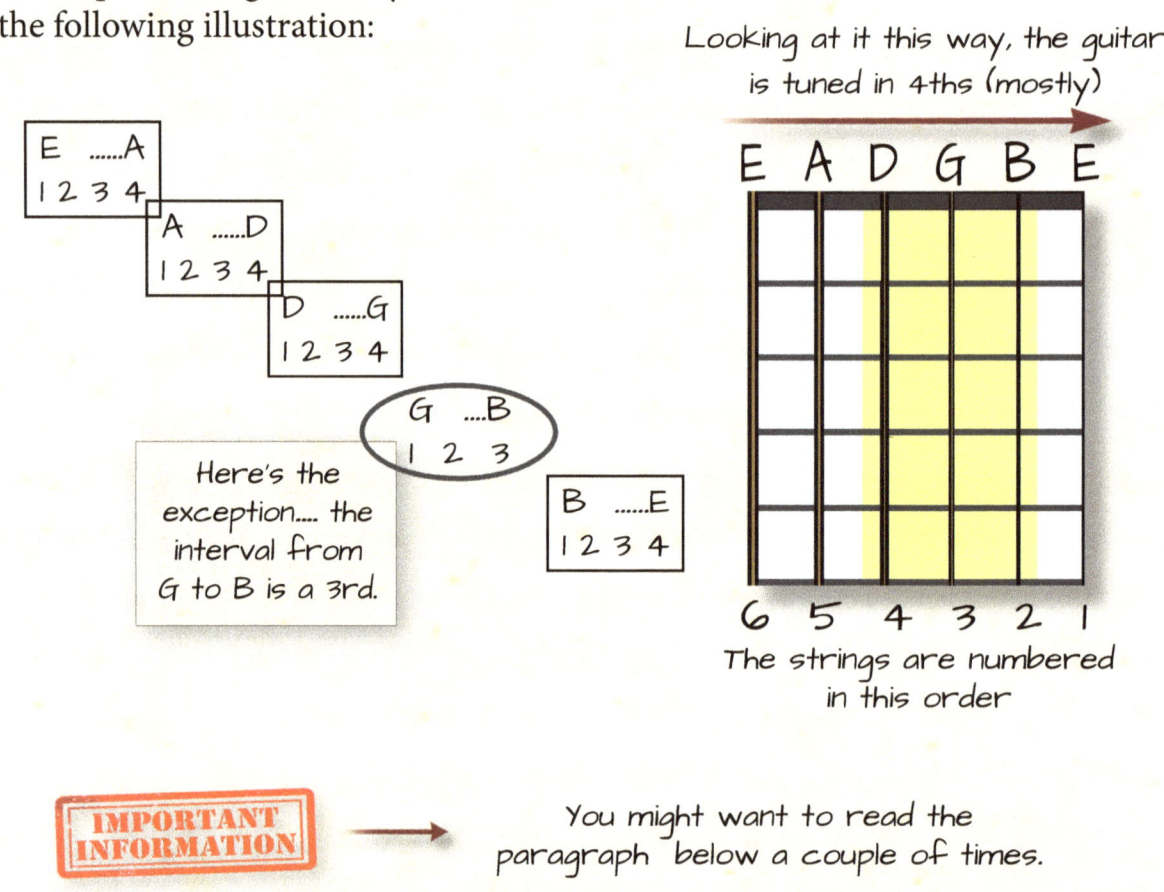

IMPORTANT INFORMATION → You might want to read the paragraph below a couple of times.

Where the strings are tuned in 4ths, we have symmetry, predictability & versatility (a large variety of notes are easy for the fingers to reach). Then when the shift takes place between the G and B strings, something very special happens... **the 2nd, 3rd & 4th strings have now become the most important strings of the instrument!** So why exactly have those strings become so important? **Because the unique tuning of these three strings creates a very unique and special group of three shapes (triads) per octave —what I call the "Cardinal Triads." These three triads/shapes are the very beginning and foundation of understanding the fretboard. They are so paramount, that I will argue that the guitar is actually a three-stringed instrument, with two auxiliary strings in the bass (E & A) and one more auxiliary string on the high end (high E). Later, when we introduce the Cardinal Triads, these three strings will be highlighted in yellow for the remainder of the book..** But before we introduce the **"Cardinal Triads"** to you, we have to make sure that you follow along and get through what's on the next few pages first...

42 Natural Notes within 12 Frets
The First Real Work to Be Done

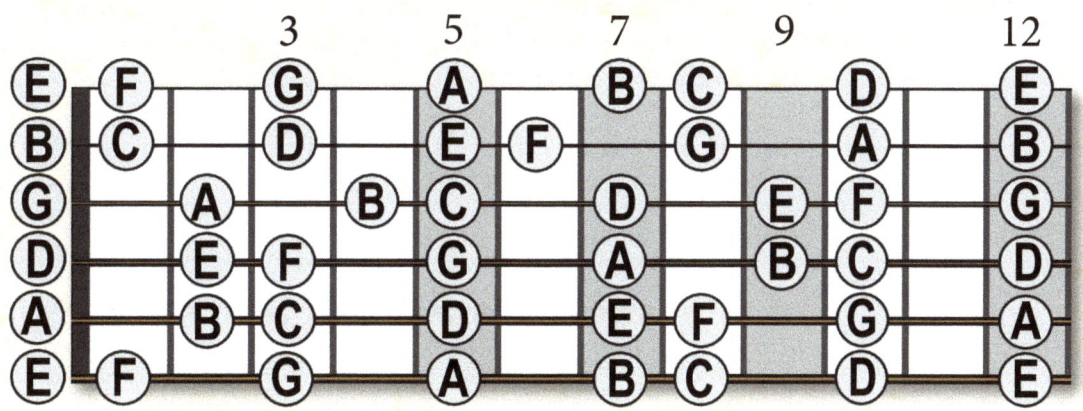

There are 42 Natural Notes between the 1st and 12th frets
(not including the sharps and flats)
7 notes on each of 6 strings. 7 X 6 = 42
48 total, if we include the notes on the open strings

The first "real work" that you're going to have to do is memorize every note on this chart. There is no getting around it... there is no other way to proceed. And there's no cute little shortcut to help you out. You just have to dig in and get it done before you move onto the next step!

I remember when I was just a boy in grammar school. We had to memorize the entire Gettysburg Address, written by President Abraham Lincoln in 1863, and then get up in front of the entire class to recite it. If it's possible for a boy so young to memorize something like that, then you can surely memorize these forty-eight notes.

If you just take five to ten minutes every morning and every evening before bedtime, it will begin sink in, deep inside your mind, probably within a few weeks. Quiz yourself every time by asking yourself where every "A" note is on every string. Then move to the "B" notes, then the "C" notes, and so on and so forth. I know it's tedious, but you *will* get through it. **When you have memorized them so well that you can point to any spot on the fretboard and easily tell yourself which note it is, then and only then you can move on to the next step!** Just concern yourself with the natural notes first... the sharps and flats between them will come easily after that.

What is a Chord
Definition and Basic Construction

A chord is a group of notes (usually three or more) played simultaneously, They most often consist of the 1st (a.k.a. Root), 3rd, and a 5th notes of the scale... and oftentimes more notes than that, adding to its complexity. Here's a simple example below in the key of C...

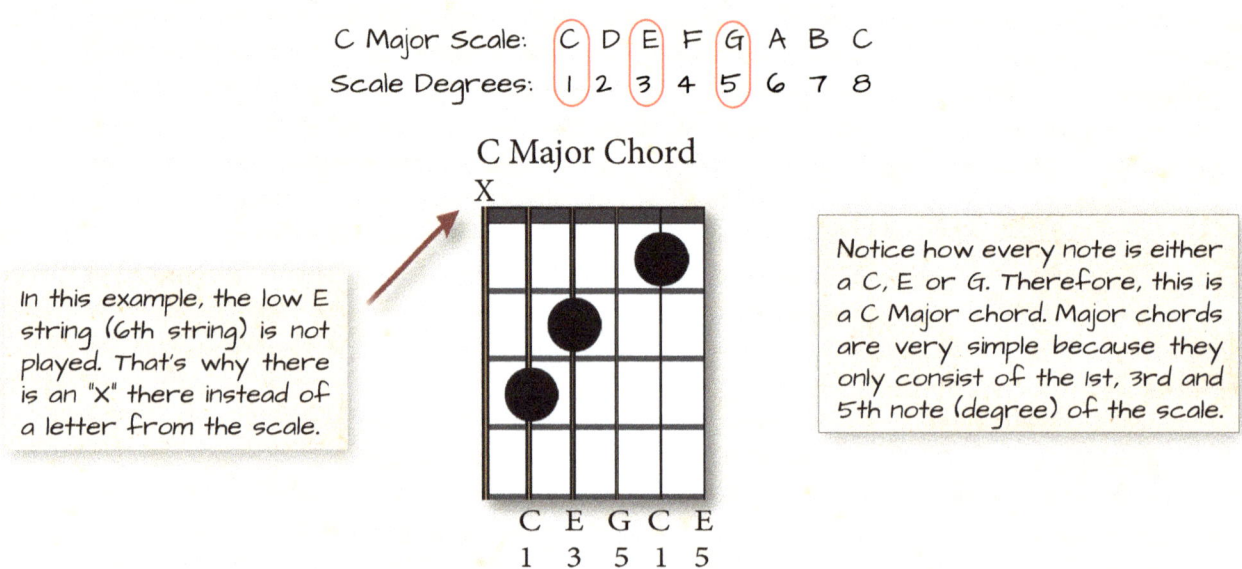

Now let's look at a couple more examples of how chords are made, this time in the key of A. First, we will write down the A Major scale, and then we will write down the scale degrees (numbers of the notes) below them.

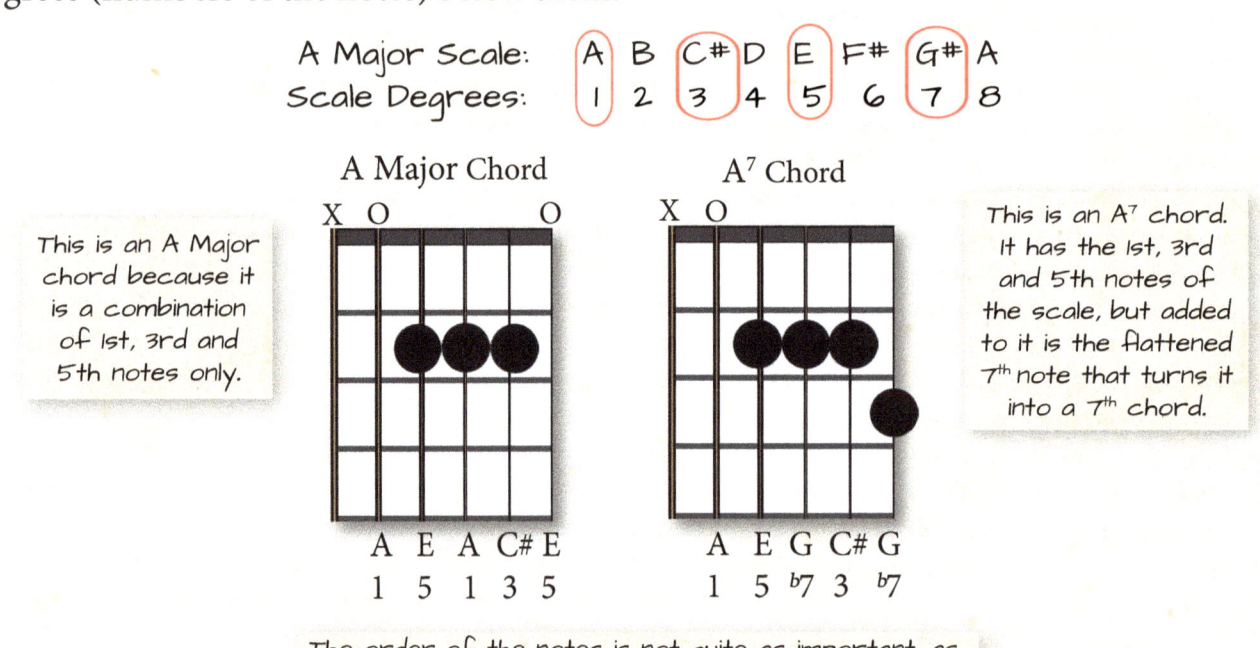

What is a Triad

A triad is a specific type of chord that has *exactly* three notes. Major Triads consist of a root (1st), 3rd & 5th, and nothing else. Triads are subsets of chords. You can think of them as the nucleus, or basic building blocks of chords. ***All triads are chords, but not all chords are triads!*** Usually, a chord has not only one, but multiple triads inside of it. Let's find just one triad in each chord below:

F Major Chord

F A C F
1 3 5 1

Looking inside a simple F Major chord, let's identify one of the triads inside of it. The triad will be three notes —a 1st (Root), 3rd and a 5th. That would be a F, A and C. So in the red square we can see one of these triads.

F Major Scale:

F G A ♭B C D E F
1 2 3 4 5 6 7 8

Triad: F - A - C

C Major Chord

C E G C E
1 3 5 1 5

Looking at the C Major chord again, let's identify one of the triads inside of the chord. The triad will be three notes —a 1st (Root), 3rd and a 5th. That would be a C, E and G. In the red square we can see one of the triads inside of this chord.

An empty circle is placed here just to illustrate where the G note is on the other side of the nut (open string in this case).

C Major Scale:

C D E F G A B C
1 2 3 4 5 6 7 8

Triad: C - E - G

A Major Chord

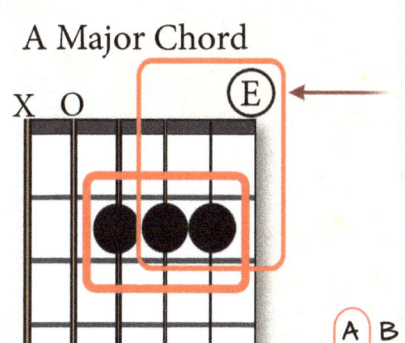

A E A C# E
1 5 1 3 5

Just for fun, let's see if we can find two triads inside of this simple A Major chord. Remember, we are looking for a combination of A, C# and E (exactly three notes to be a triad).

The empty circle is where the E note is on the other side of the nut (open string).

A Major Scale:

A B C# D E F# G# A
1 2 3 4 5 6 7 8

Triad: A - C# - E

Introducing the Three Cardinal Triads

Shown in the three illustrations below, are the three most important, "Cardinal Triad" shapes to learn. They are located on the three most important strings (highlighted in yellow from here on out). We'll learn these first, and how to use them. Then later, we will "branch out" onto the rest of the strings (auxiliary strings) and see how the shapes grow.

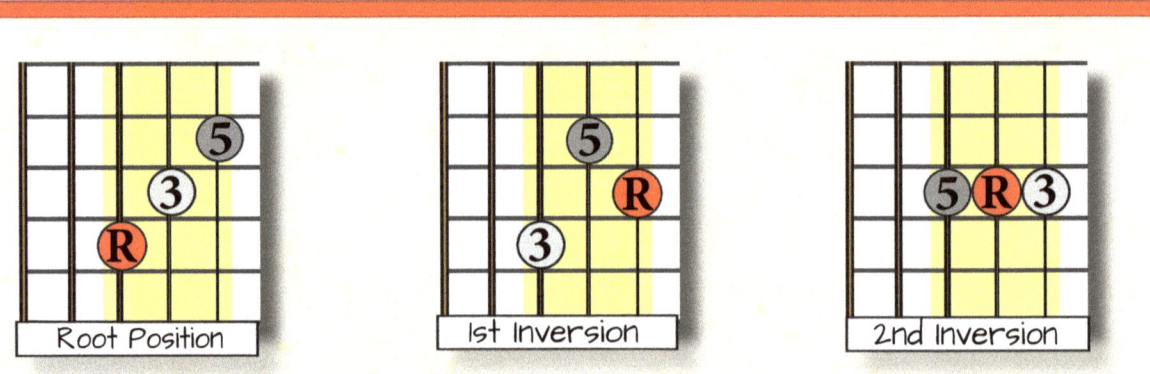

The three "Cardinal Triads" sit on the three most important strings. These Shapes are the foundation that everything else will be built upon! Everything that you play is to be seen as an extension of one of these. They are the central spine—the Axis Mundi. We now begin to learn HOW TO LOOK through the Lens and SEE the fretboard.

Looking at these diagrams, "R" is the root note, (first note of the scale). The "3" is the third note and the "5" is the fifth note of the scale. *The Root Position shape* has the root note on the bass string. *The 1st Inversion shape* has the root on the treble (high) string. The *2nd Inversion shape* has the root on the middle string. Always be mindful of where the root is —which string, which fret, and also which note it is. The root dictates the key of the triad/chord*!* That's why you had to memorize the 42/48 notes of the fretboard first. Capisce?

Each one of these triads is a movable shape. They can be moved to anywhere on the fretboard (on these 3 strings) to create a different chord, or to create the same chord in a different location (using a different inversion) on the fretboard (which in turn, renders a different "voicing").

Take notice that each one of the Cardinal Triads (their shapes) look very similar to some of the basic beginner chords that you already know. Take a moment to look at them closely, and familiarize yourself with them... If you add one note to the root position triad it *could* be an F chord (depending on what the root note is, or where it's placed on the fretboard). The 2nd inversion triad already looks exactly *like* the shape of an A chord. The 1st inversion triad *could* be a basic D chord if you added one more note to it.

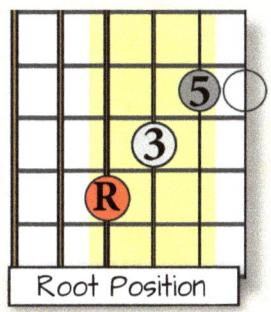

Root Position

Looking at the diagram to the left, you can see how the Root Position triad looks a lot like a basic F chord if you were to add that other note onto the first string. It can move up or down the neck to create a different chord/key.

The Second Inversion shape already looks exactly like a basic A chord. You can place it anywhere on the neck. Always focus on the Root note, because that will determine the chord or key that you're playing.

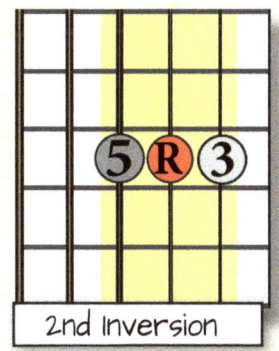

2nd Inversion

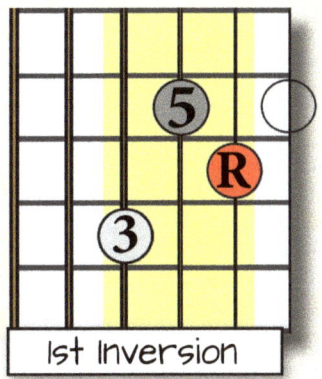

1st Inversion

The First Inversion Shape can look just like a basic D chord if you were to add that other note onto the first string. Again, when you play this shape, focus on the root note. Always identify the root note! It will give you your bearings, so you always know exactly where you are and what you are playing.

Again, these three highlighted shapes are the **"Cardinal Triads."** Every other structure on the fretboard is born from them — all other forms are simply extensions or modifications of these three. You will soon see how.

Now let's put these triad/shapes into action and see how they work. If we designate the root note as an "A," we can create some simple three-note "A" chords with our triads.

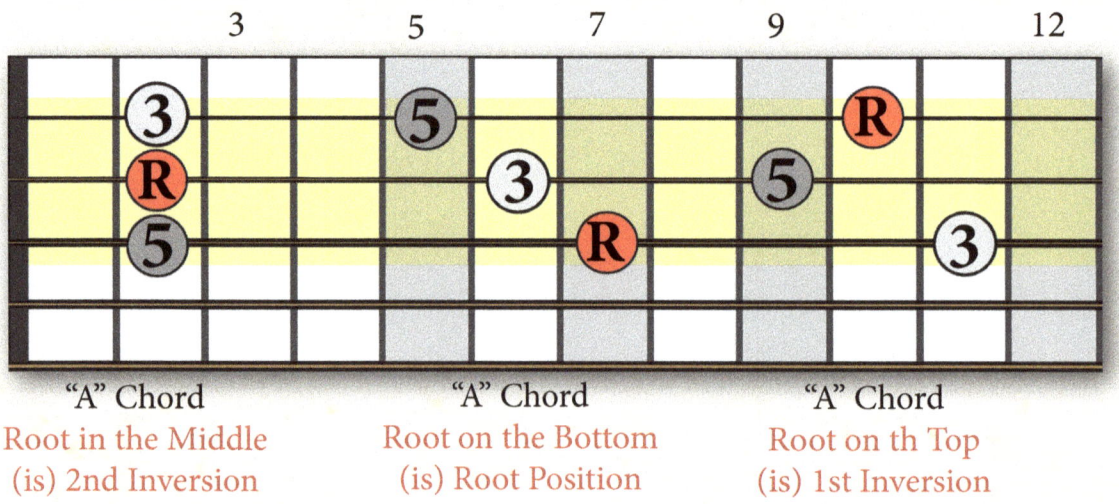

"A" Chord
Root in the Middle
(is) 2nd Inversion

"A" Chord
Root on the Bottom
(is) Root Position

"A" Chord
Root on th Top
(is) 1st Inversion

This is the natural order of the Cardinal Triads on the fretboard. Three inversions per octave... (5th, R, 3rd... R, 3rd, 5th... 3rd, 5th, R). They just keep repeating, endlessly spiraling upward through the higher octaves... Can you can find the next "A" chord on the 14th fret of your guitar? Hint: Follow the pattern... It will be a 2nd inversion shape. Always, always, always **look for and study the shapes and patterns!!!**

Take some time to play around with these three triad inversions, one after the other so they sound good together. Get very familiar and comfortable with them. Notice that there are three inversions/shapes per octave. Listen to the different voicings they have. Substitute them into some of your favorite songs. Don't be in a hurry... it's best if you take a lot of time to play around with these shapes before we move on. Give it enough time to sink in well! Then on the next page, we'll move the shapes around a little bit more.

A world (whirled) of inversions

Take a look below and see how each Cardinal Triad can be moved around, thereby changing the keys of the chords. Keep your attention on the Root note... it defines the chord. Below are just a *few* examples. There are many more possibilities...

If we take our 2nd Inversion A Major triad and move it up to the 7th fret, it becomes a D Major triad. If we move it up to the 12th fret, it becomes a G Major triad. Follow the root note because it defines the key of the chord. Can you tell me what it would be on the 9th fret?

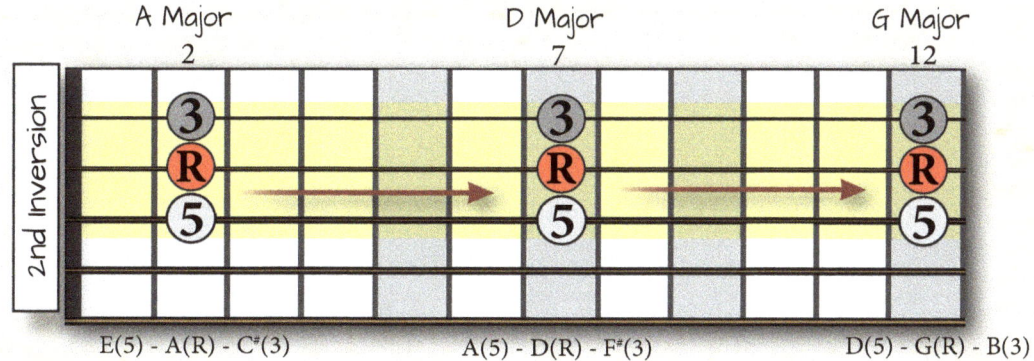

The Root Position A Major triad on the 7th fret can slide down to a G Major triad on the 5th fret, or slide up to a C Major triad on the 10th fret. What would it be if you slid down the neck and put the root on the 3rd fret?

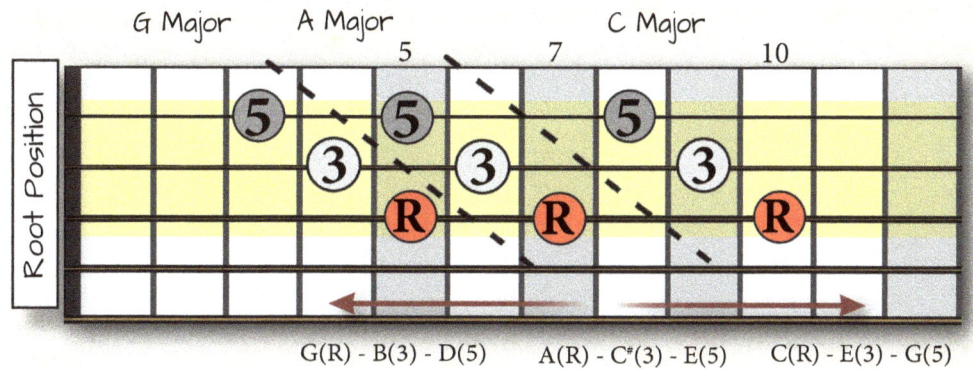

The 1st inversion A Major on the 10th fret can slide down to an F Major on the 6th fret, or all the way down to a D Major on the 3rd fret. Let the Root guide you. What key would you be in if you put the root on the 8th fret?

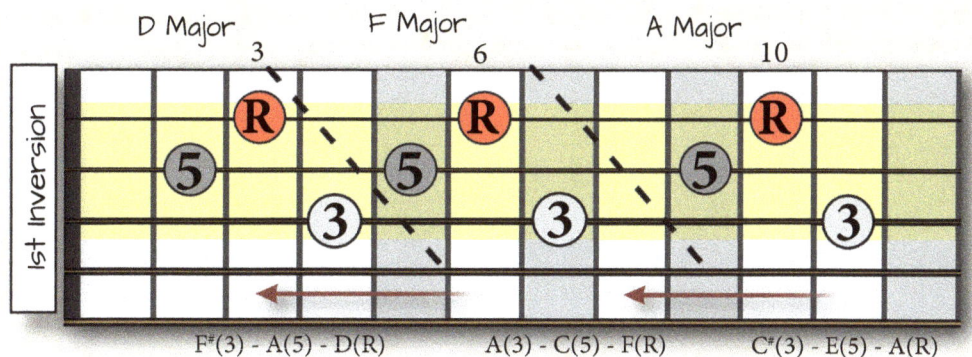

Here's a little chord progression you can do to help you practice the Cardinal Triad shapes. It's a very basic I - IV - V progression, but uses different inversions on different parts of the neck. I'm a finger-stylist, so I like to pluck the strings with my fingers and push out a few melodies along the way, but you can also simply strum it just as well. Have some fun with it while you're learning. Feel free to explore and mix it up, too.

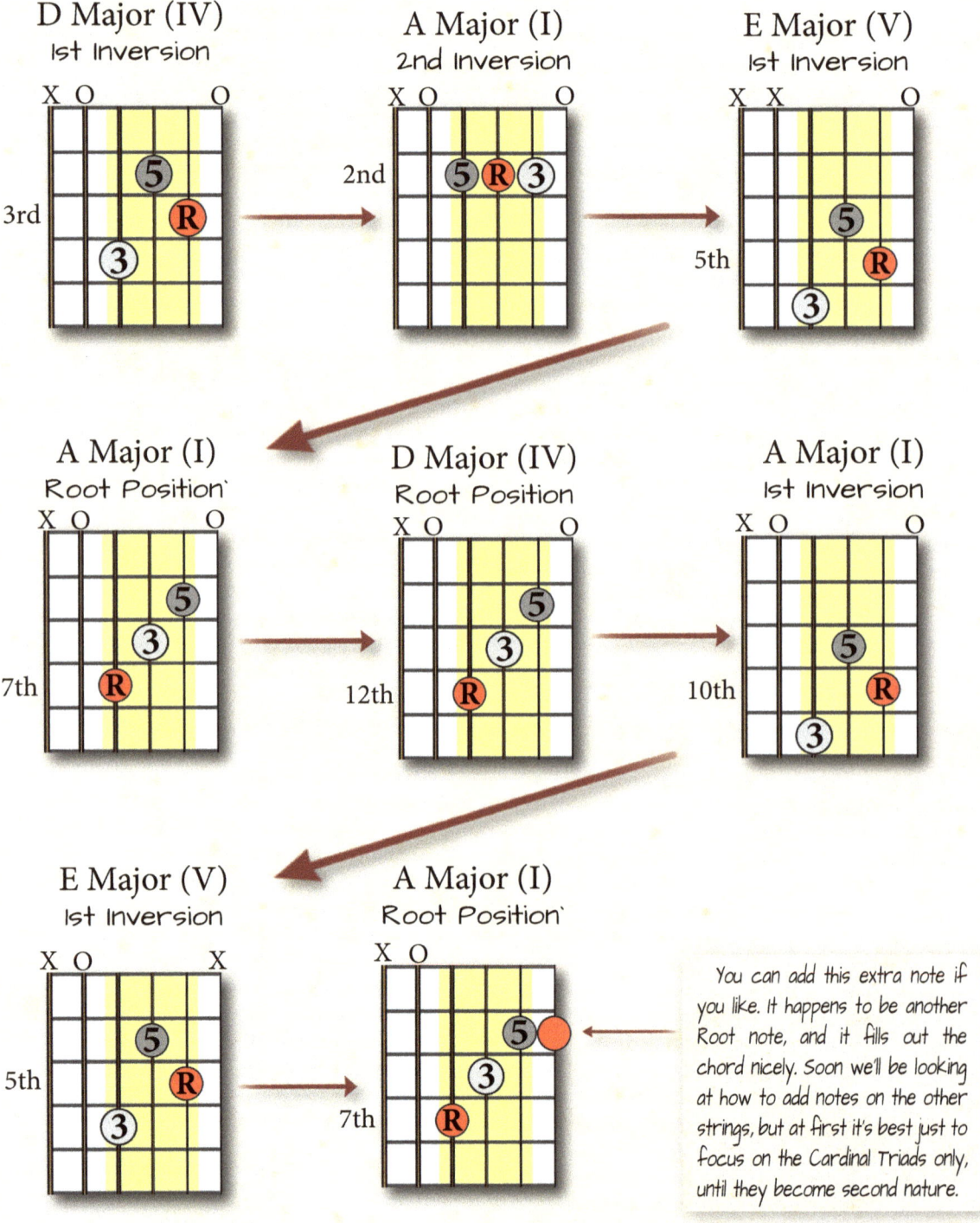

13

Review
Making the Major Cardinal Triads

Time for a quick review and quiz using what you've learned so far. Upon the illustrations on the following page, draw circles where the Root, 3rd and 5th are to be on the fretboard. As an example, I'll do the first one for you here...

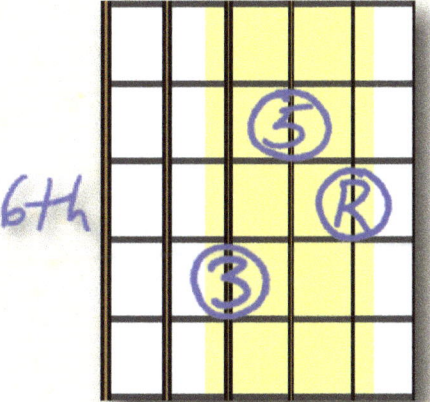

Create a 1st Inversion F Major triad

"1st Inversion" tells you which shape that you'll be using, and also which string that the root is on.

Because it's a 1st inversion, you will find the root note (F) on the second string. And because you have memorized your 42/48 notes, you know that the second string F note is on the sixth fret. Then, using that note as the root, form a 1st inversion shape over the 2nd, 3rd and 4th strings.

Now give it a try on your guitar. Get familiar with this shape and how this particular voicing feels and sounds. See if you can substitute one of the F chords in a song you know with this F triad/chord. Neil Young, as an example, used it for the intro to his song "Old Man." If you want to fill out the chord a little bit more, you can add more notes... maybe try to add another "F" note on the fifth string, or another "A" note on the first string. We will learn more about adding those other notes soon.

"Music is my religion."
— Jimi Hendrix

Review Quiz

Now it's your turn... create the chord/triads on the charts below. Don't peek at the answers on the following page until after you're done.

Create a Root Position, A Major triad (Root in the bass, the 4th string)

Create a 1st Inversion D Major triad (Root on the high end, 2nd string)

Create a 2nd Inversion C Major triad (Root in the middle, the 3rd string)

Create a Root Position D Major triad (Root in the bass, the 4th string)

Create a 2nd Inversion E Major triad (Root in the middle, on the 3rd string)

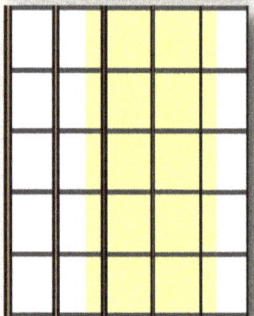

Create a 1st Inversion A Major triad (Root on the high end, the 2nd string)

The light of the body is the eye:
if therefore thine eye be single, thy whole body shall be full of light.
— Matthew 6:22-23 KJV

Answers to the Quiz

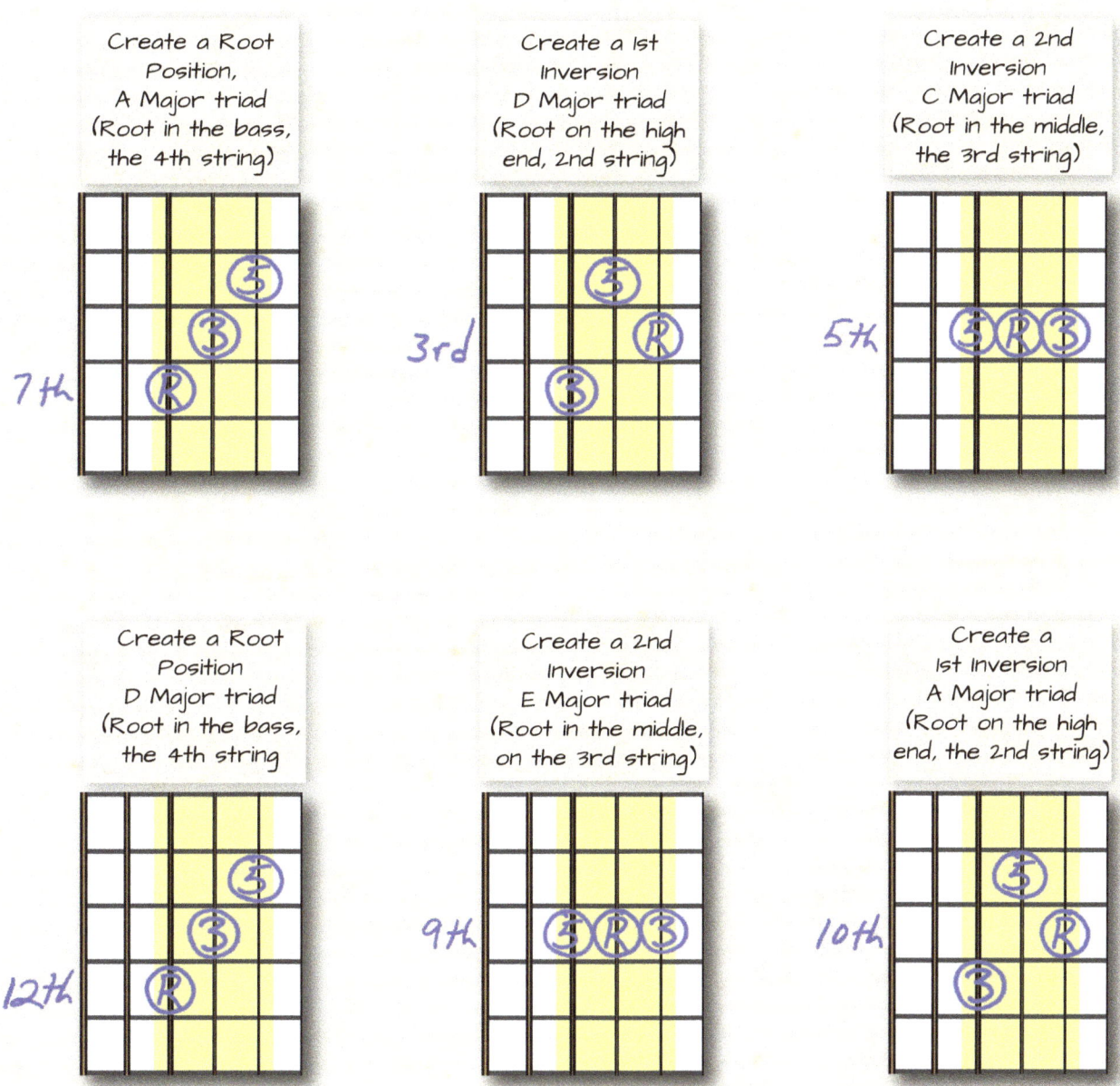

Play these shapes on your guitar and make them your own by weaving them into songs you already know. Remember, every one of these chords is movable: shift it to a new fret, and the root changes; a new chord is born. Explore the neck. Let your hands travel. Listen as each new position reveals a new key. On the next page, we'll expand these triads onto the other strings and begin to see the larger architecture of the fretboard.

Expanding the Triad Shapes
Moving onto the Auxiliary Strings

By now, you know what chords and triads are, and the difference between them. You also learned about the three Cardinal Triad shapes and how they sit on the 2nd, 3rd and 4th strings (the most important strings, highlighted in yellow). But now let's get a little deeper into it. Let's expand those patterns to the rest of the strings as well. The patterns shown below are the FULL (Major) patterns... there are three of them. Every three consecutive notes (within each pattern) form a separate triad to be learned. That makes four triads within each one of the three patterns, rendering a total of *twelve* triads in all (4 x 3 = 12).

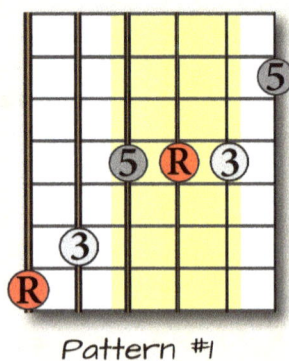
Pattern #1

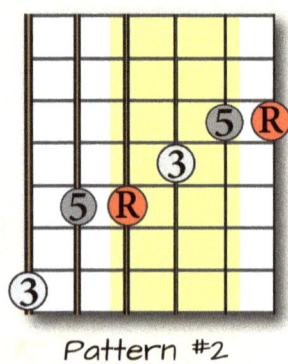
Pattern #2

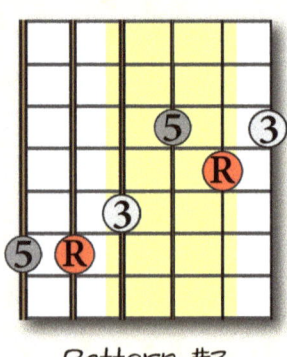
Pattern #3

The Three FULL Triadic Patterns (Major)
Every three consecutive notes form a Major triad with a Root, 3rd & 5th, but in a different order (inversion) each time. There are twelve in all.
See if you can identify each inversion inside each of the three patterns above.

...the illustration below shows the same three (movable) patterns again, but it shows them together in their natural order upon the fretboard

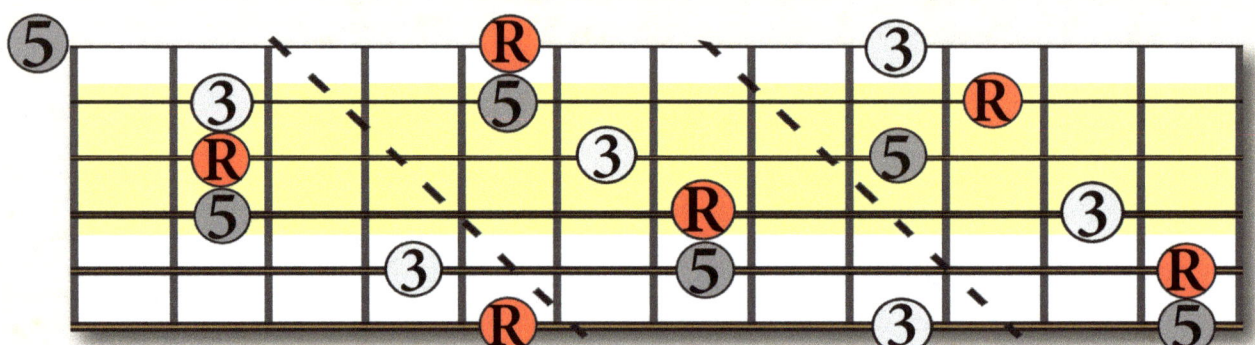

This pattern keeps repeating and spiraling up through every octave above... to infinity and beyond!

17

Individually Separating the Expanded Shapes
(for Further Elucidation)

Down below are the same three full patterns again, but this time they're each separated into four individual triads. Become very familiar with all twelve triad shapes and how they fit together and blend into one another on the fretboard. Always remember which note in each triad is the root.

Each triad is but an inversion of the others in its own pattern... either **Root position** (where the root is on the bottom/bass), **1st inversion** (where the root is on the top/high end), or **2nd inversion** (where the root is in the middle). Once all of the Major triads are memorized, they can then be easily modified into any type of chord you wish with the simple knowledge of chord construction.

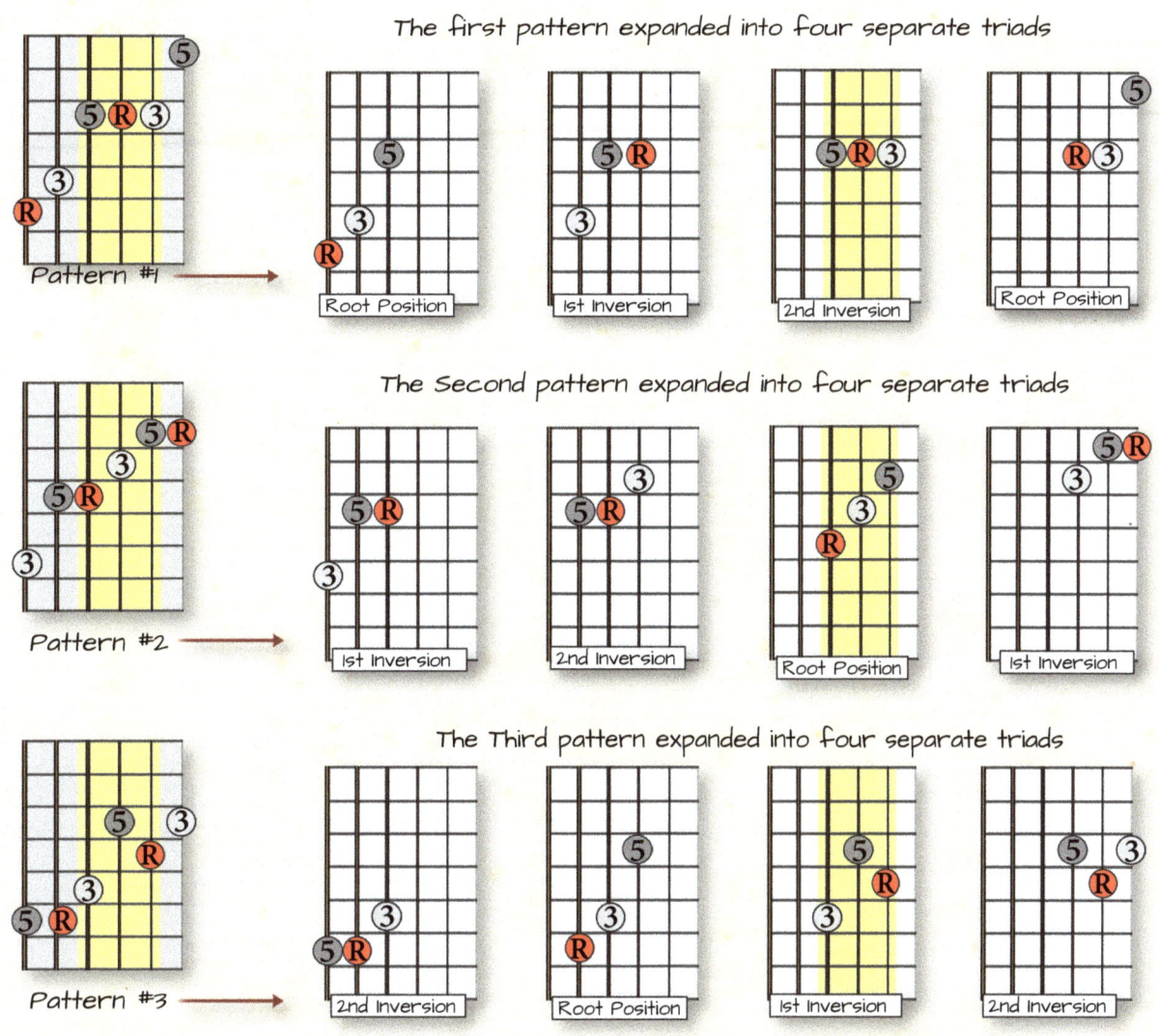

Notice that in the illustrations above, the Cardinal Triads are highlighted.

Making a Chord Shape from Pattern #3

You can play the individual triads like you play chords, if you can silence or dampen the other strings. But you can also use the other strings to fill in the chord if you know which notes to use. So let's try something... let's merge a few of the triads to create a more complete chord that can be moved to different locations along the neck. For this example, we'll take these three triads from Pattern #3...

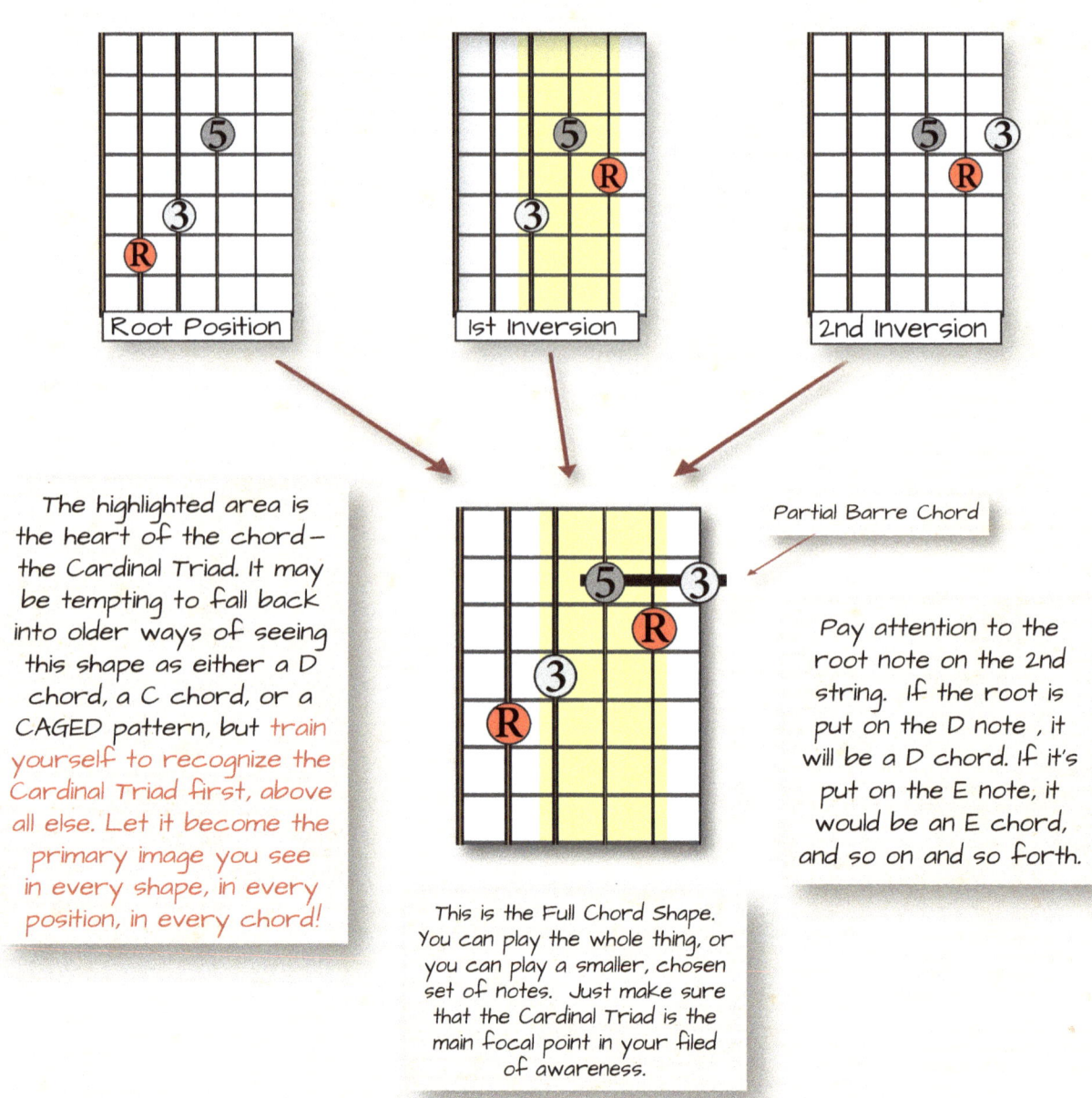

The highlighted area is the heart of the chord — the Cardinal Triad. It may be tempting to fall back into older ways of seeing this shape as either a D chord, a C chord, or a CAGED pattern, but train yourself to recognize the Cardinal Triad first, above all else. Let it become the primary image you see in every shape, in every position, in every chord!

This is the Full Chord Shape. You can play the whole thing, or you can play a smaller, chosen set of notes. Just make sure that the Cardinal Triad is the main focal point in your filed of awareness.

Pay attention to the root note on the 2nd string. If the root is put on the D note, it will be a D chord. If it's put on the E note, it would be an E chord, and so on and so forth.

Always look for and see the patterns in music... I assure you, they are everywhere! The entire universe, in fact, is woven into some kind of cosmic pattern, of which music is a direct reflection. Or, depending on how you want to look at it, perhaps the universe is just a reflection of the music.

Making a Chord Shape from Pattern #2

In this example below, three of the triads from Pattern #2 have been merged.

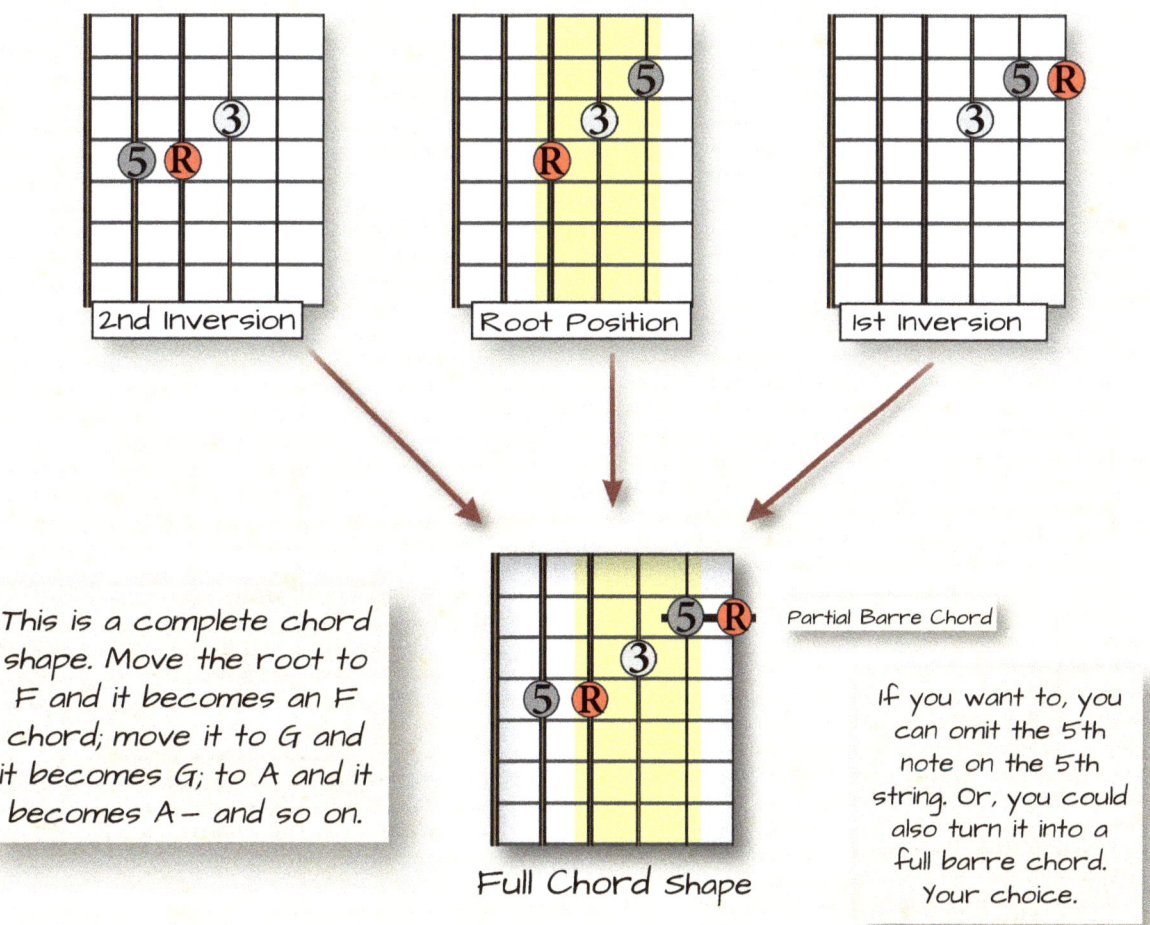

This is a complete chord shape. Move the root to F and it becomes an F chord; move it to G and it becomes G; to A and it becomes A – and so on.

If you want to, you can omit the 5th note on the 5th string. Or, you could also turn it into a full barre chord. Your choice.

Wherever the root goes, the chord follows. For this reason, your attention should remain anchored on the root of the Cardinal Triad. (Good thing you've memorized your 42/48 notes.) You may recognize this form as part of the familiar F barre chord you learned as a beginner, but train your eye to see the Cardinal Triad first and foremost. The Cardinal Triad is the Lens through which the fretboard begins to reveal itself.

"Psychedelic vision is reality to me and always was."
— John Lennon, September 1968

Making a Chord Shape from Pattern #1

Lastly, let's use the triads from Pattern #1 to make some chord shapes. There are a few ways that this can be done, depending on the kind of voicing you prefer.

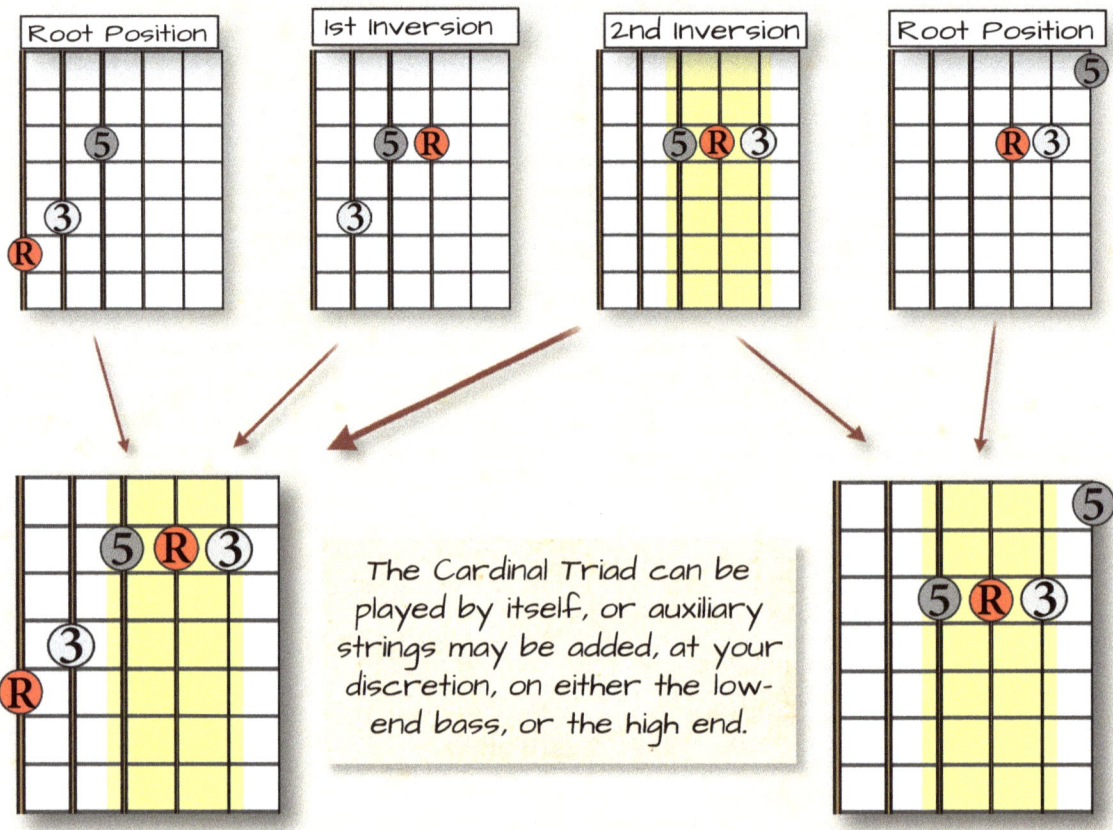

The Cardinal Triad can be played by itself, or auxiliary strings may be added, at your discretion, on either the low-end bass, or the high end.

I would like to mention that there is another chord shape that I find useful with this Cardinal Triad, but it isn't entirely created with Pattern #1. It's a kind of hybrid... it uses the Cardinal Triad from Pattern #1, but adds one or two of the bass strings from Pattern #3 ...this is but **one of many examples** of how chords are created from blending the different patterns. If you look closely, you might also be able to see a very common barre chord and/or a power chord inside of this shape. This is illustrated below:

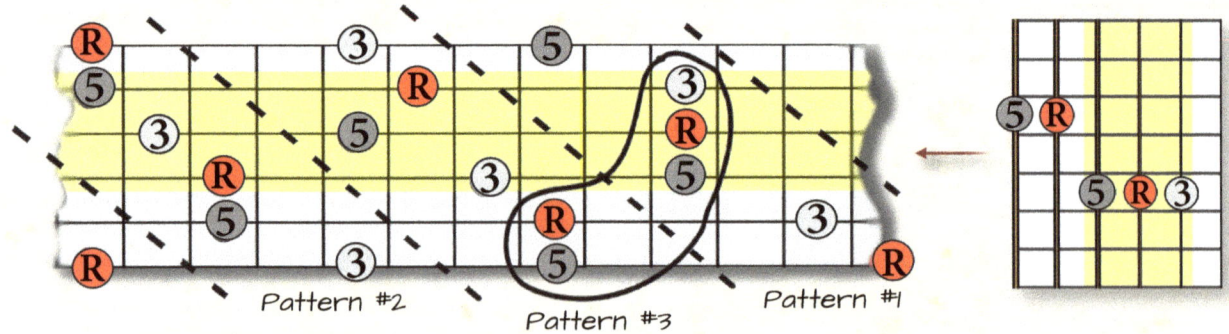

Making the (m)inor Triads
The Beauty of Sadness

If you have come this far and memorized the 42/48 notes and the twelve Major triad shapes within the first twelve frets, you can pat yourself on the back—you've passed a HUGE milestone. From now on, it's about learning how to modify and build upon these shapes, using the Cardinal Triads as reference points on the fretboard. **Now hear this: There are four fundamental qualities a triad can take on: Major, minor, augmented, and diminished.** The first of these four that we'll be exploring are the minor triads. The logic is simple—flatten the 3rd degree. In the illustration below, the empty circles mark where the 3rd notes of the original Major triad used to be, giving you a clear point of reference for the change.

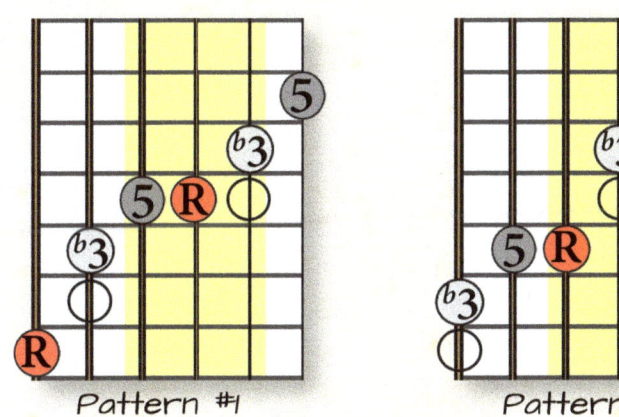

Pattern #1   Pattern #2   Pattern #3

Looking at just the three Cardinal Triads (on strings 2, 3 and 4), you probably notice something familiar about these minor shapes. You can probably see a basic Am chord shape in pattern #1. If you put the root note of Pattern #2 on the 7th fret (4th string), you have another Am chord. If you put the root note of pattern #3 on the 10th fret (2nd string), you have the Am chord again. So if we wanted to make a Dm chord somewhere on the fretboard, with a Cardinal Triad on the 2nd, 3rd and 4th strings, where would we put it? Hint: use the Root note of the triad; place the root note where the "D" note is. Are you starting to "get it" yet? Are you starting to SEE it?

I think that Michelangelo should have put those musical notes in there when he painted the ceiling of the Sistine Chapel (1508-1512).

*To be a great musician, four things are needed. Physical ability, mental prowess, a bold heart, and last but definitely not least... That secret special something that **finds you** only when you're ready.*

22

The (m)inor Triads Expanded

The illustration below shows the three full minor patterns spread out in their natural order upon the 12 frets of the fretboard. Learn to see each individual triad and how they flow and blend into one another. Recognize where the root is in each shape and which inversion it is. You can change keys by simply repositioning the same shape to a different location on the fretboard (and the root note defines the key). Play around with it until you find some shapes that feel natural and comfortable under your fingers.

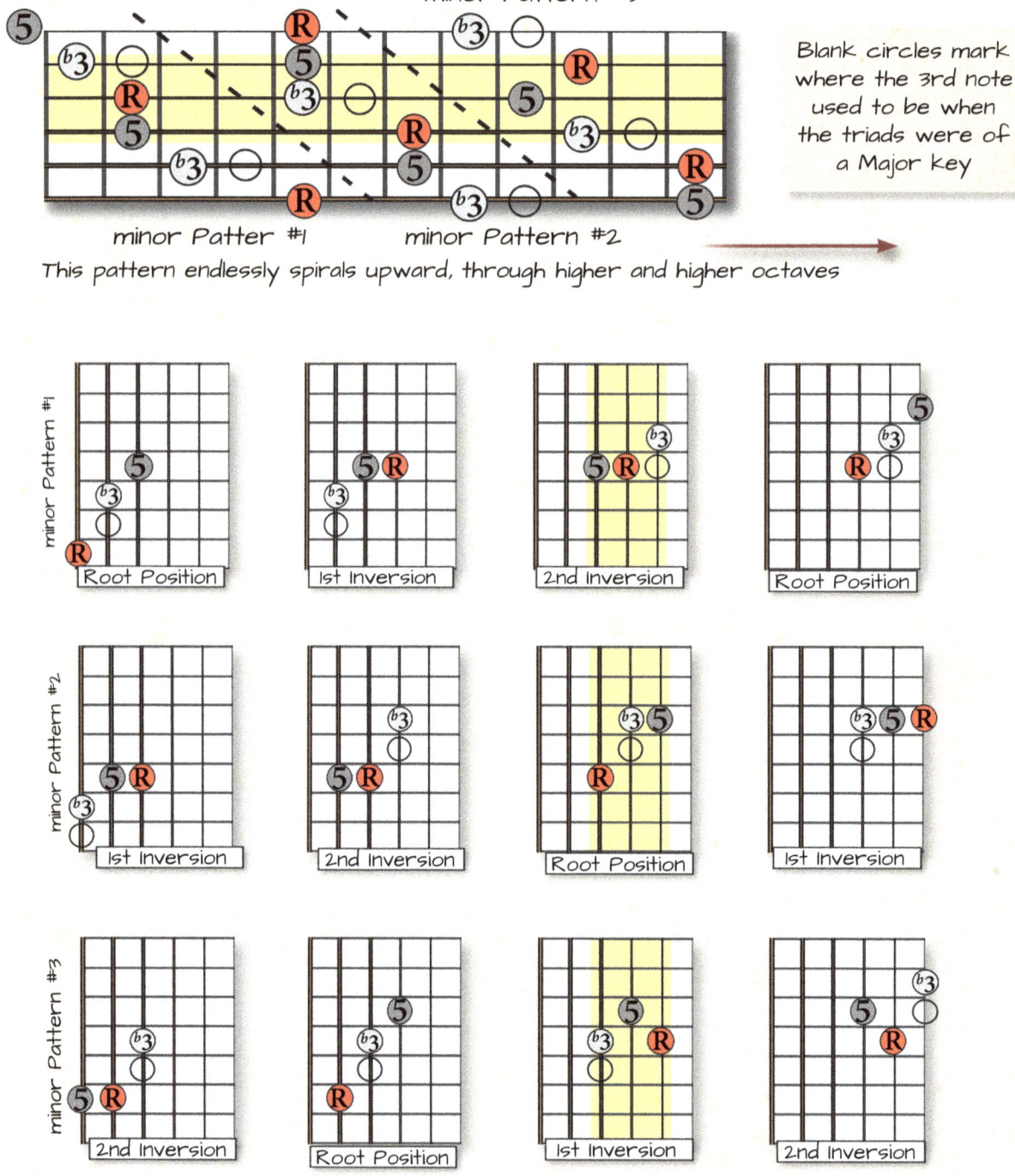

Augmented Triads

Augmented chords are created by raising the 5th note by a half step (one fret). The sound they create is unsettling, ambiguous and dreamy. They seem to bend or blur the tonal center of gravity, while pulling you to the next chord, *forcing the ear to interpret or choose the root based on the surrounding harmony.*

See if you can find some popular songs that have Augmented chords in them. Listen to them closely; identify them, how they are used, and the function they serve.

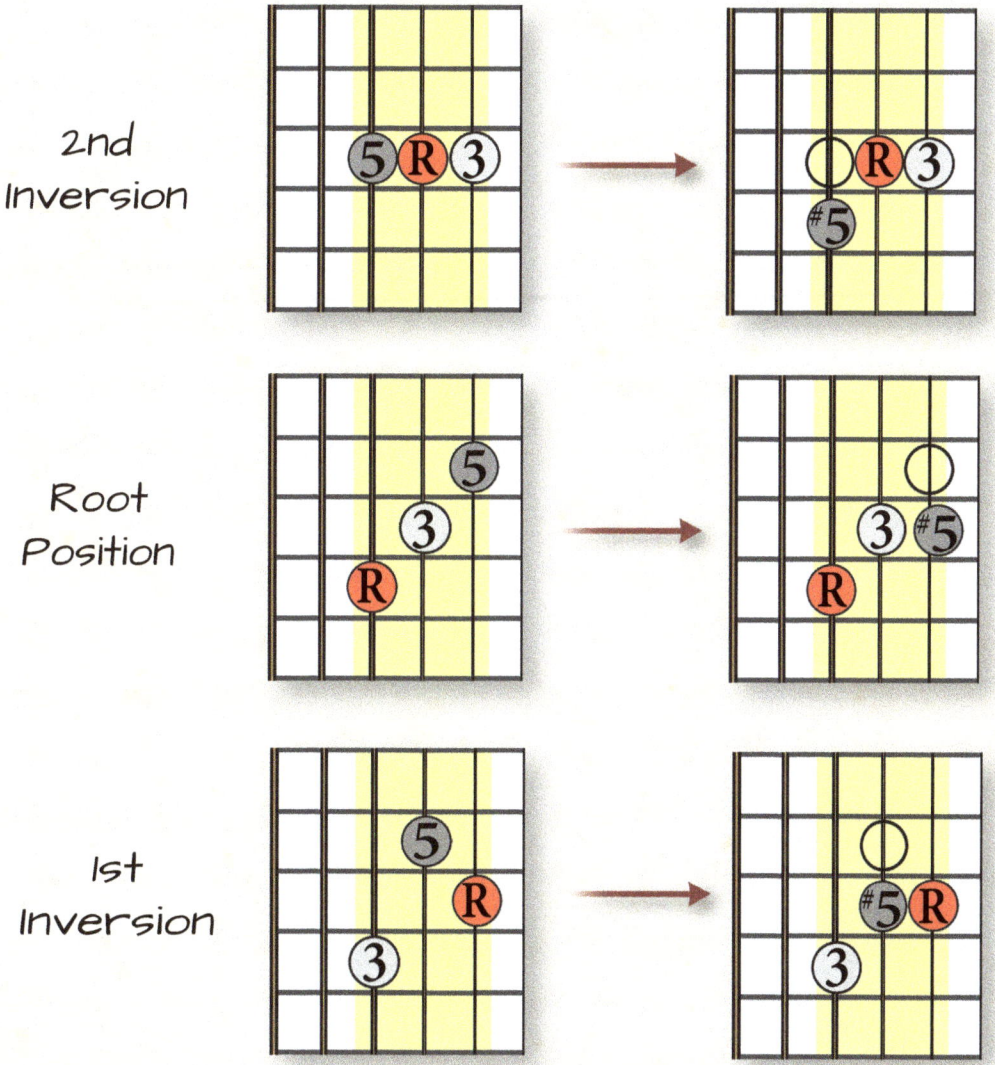

Do you notice something unique and interesting here? Every single inversion of the Augmented triads takes the same shape! What in the "whirled" is going on here? Let's look at this some more...

Let's assign our augmented Cardinal Triads to the key of A major. The blank circles indicate where the 5th note of the original major triad once appeared, just to serve as a point of reference. As you can see, each inversion has transformed into the same shape, but sits on a different location on the neck. Move the shape up and down the neck a few times and get used to the way they feel and sound. The sound may feel a little awkward at first until you get more familiar with them and learn how to use them.

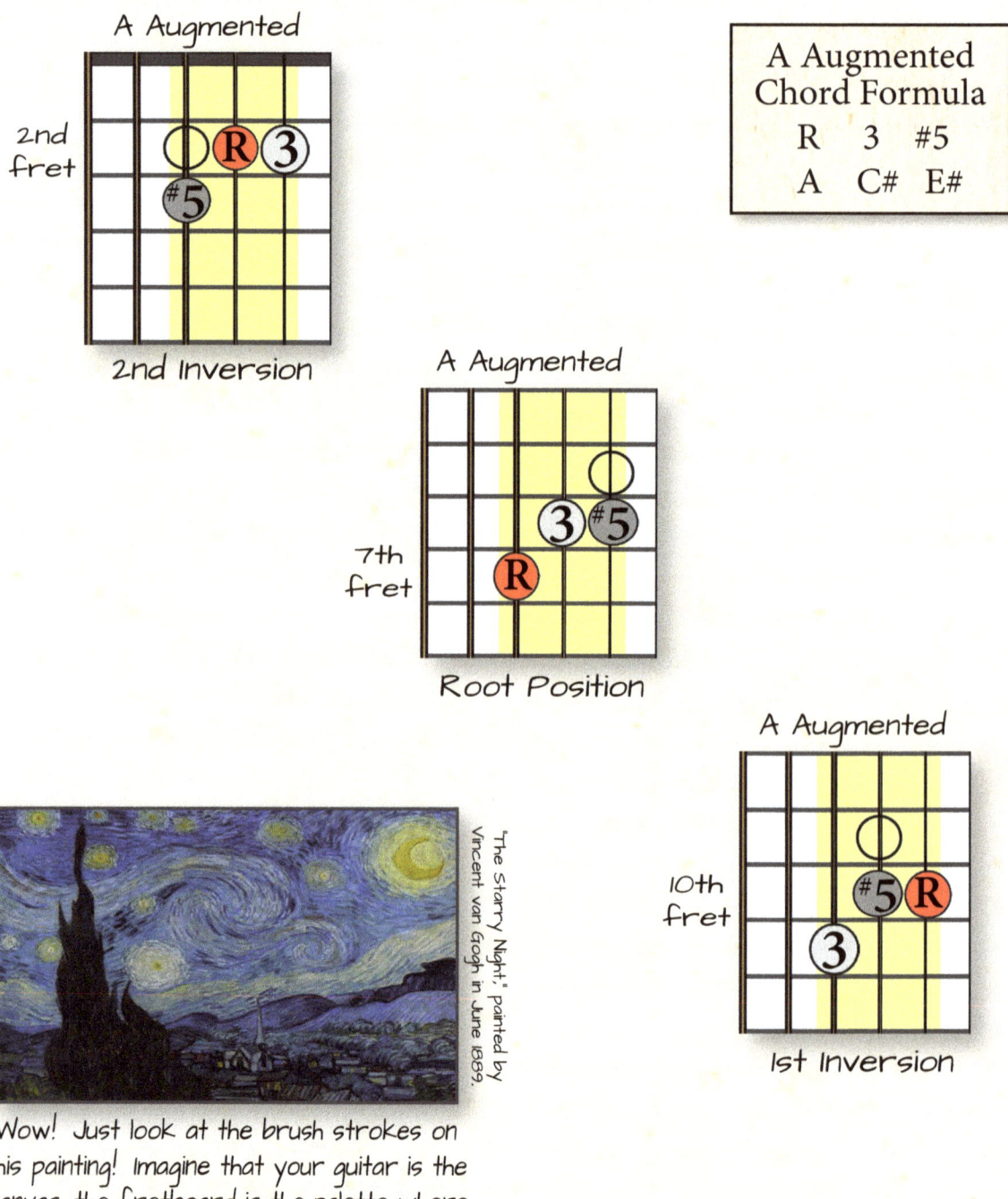

Wow! Just look at the brush strokes on this painting! Imagine that your guitar is the canvas, the fretboard is the palette where the colors are mixed, and your right hand controls the brush strokes upon the strings.

Let's conduct a little experiment here: if we move our triads to a different set of strings, will the same thing happen? Will the other Augmented triads take the same shape again? Let's find out... but this time, let's try it with C augmented.

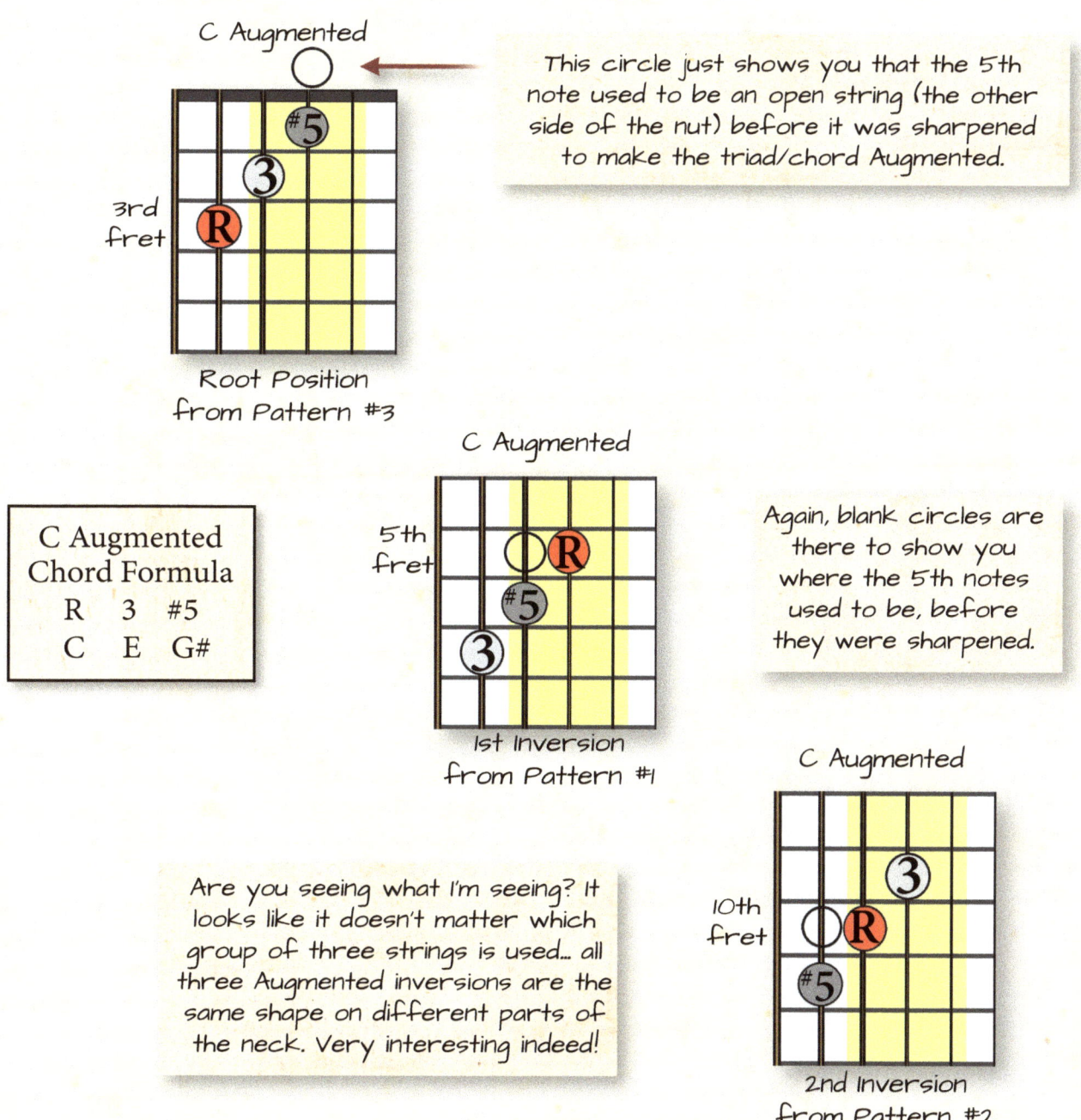

The artist is the antidote to the self-limiting, soul-destroying systems around us. "...art's task is to save the soul of mankind. And that anything less is a dithering while Rome burns. Because if the artists, who are self-selected for being able to journey into the other, cannot find the way, then the way cannot be found."
—Terrence McKenna

Augmented triads are also known as "symmetrical" triads. One of their magical qualities is that any note in the triad can serve as the root; the actual root is determined by the musical context.

Now, let's merge and blend the augmented triad shapes from different string groups, just as we did with the other triads, to see the larger chord shapes that emerge. Because any note can function as the root, the charts will use only red circles to mark the triad notes. We'll explore this phenomenon in more detail on the next page.

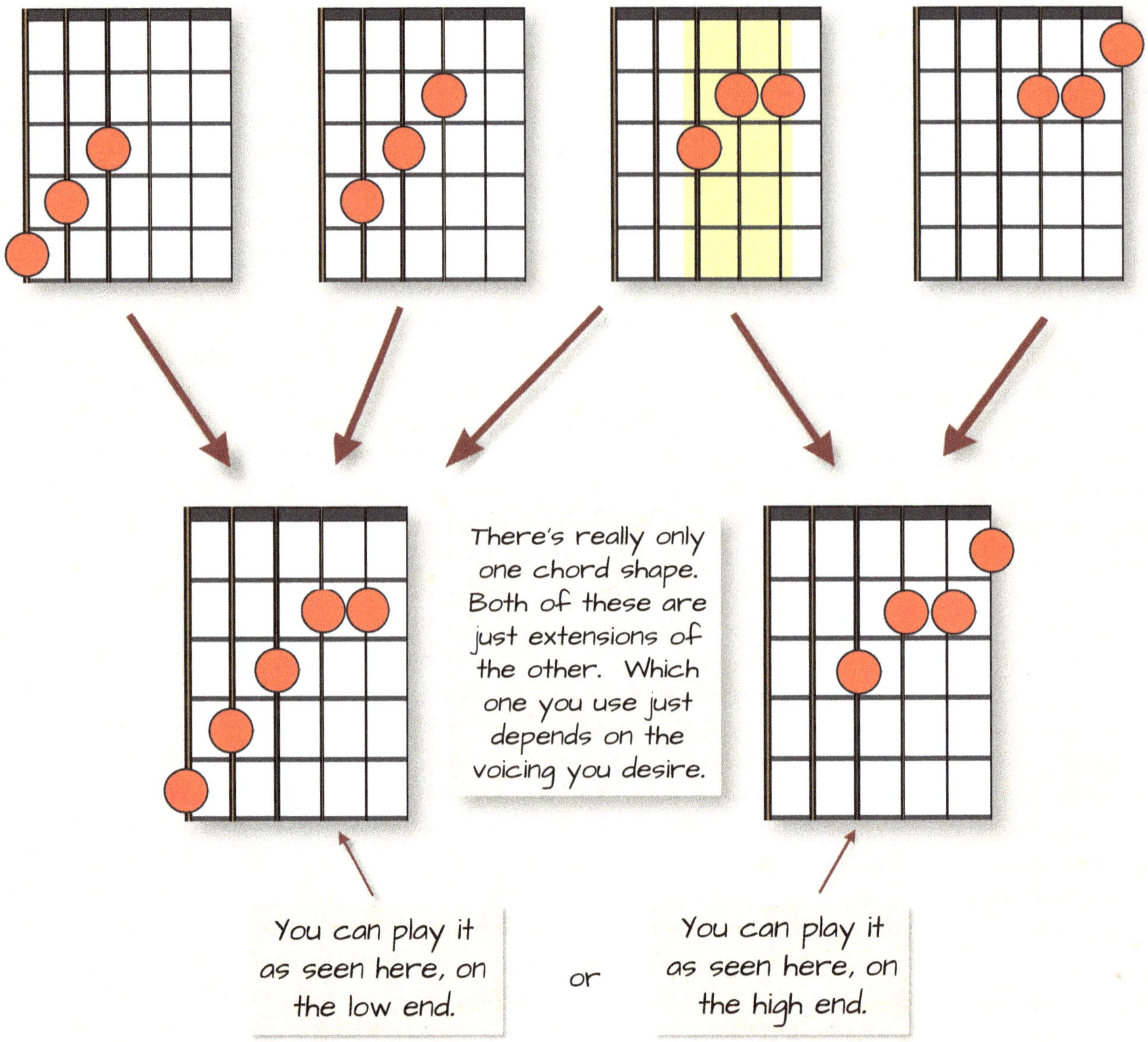

There's really only one chord shape. Both of these are just extensions of the other. Which one you use just depends on the voicing you desire.

You can play it as seen here, on the low end.

or

You can play it as seen here, on the high end.

Rhythm is the blood — the living force that moves through you from the unseen world around you. Let it flow freely through your body and into your instrument. More important than choosing the right note to play is that the rhythm itself is alive within you.

Augmented triads are built from stacked Major third intervals, dividing the octave into three equal parts. Study the symmetry in the image below. As you can see, there are only four augmented triads, and each one can be named three different ways (one for each note). The one chord shape covers all twelve keys, depending on where it's placed on the neck.

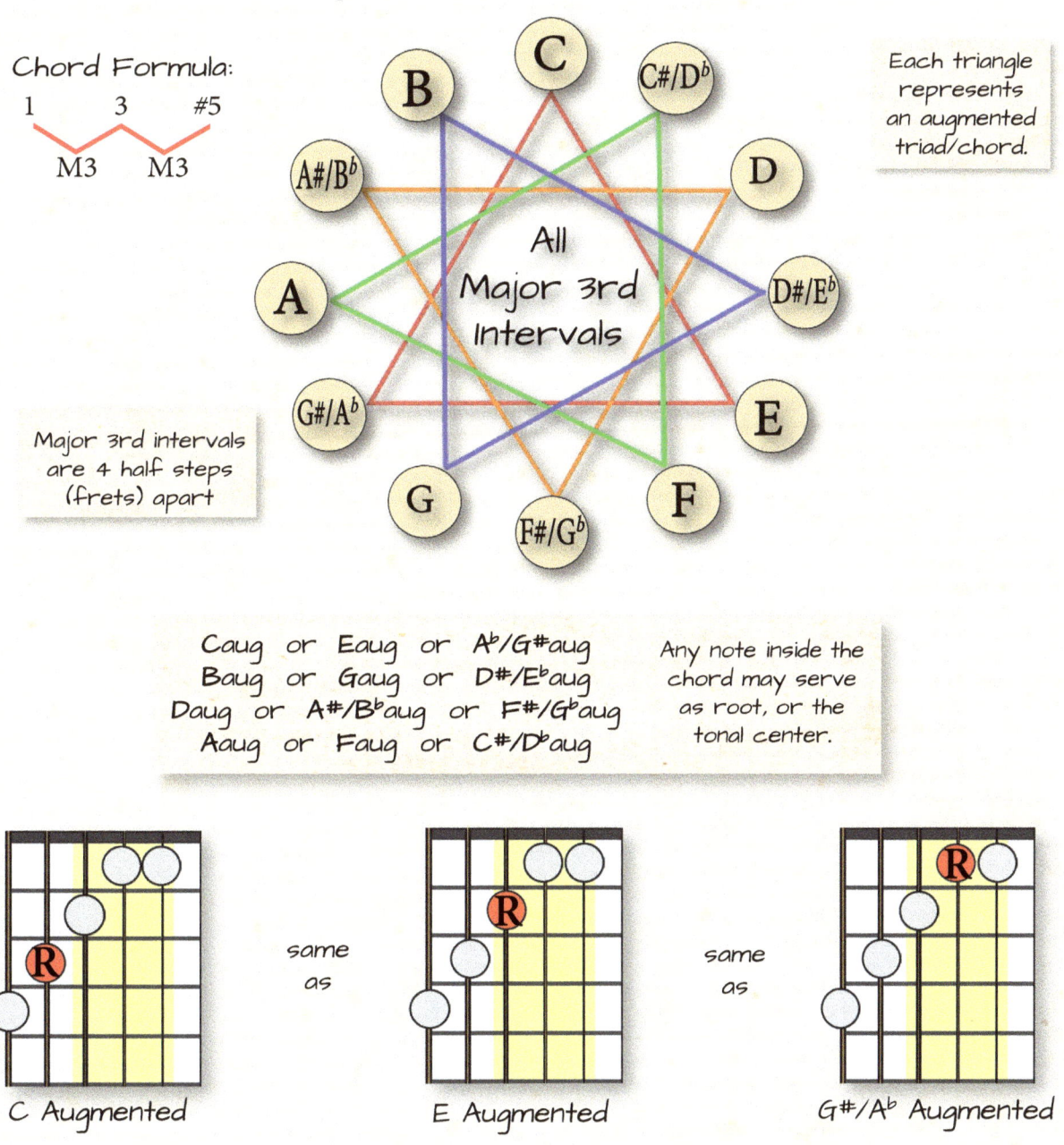

This shape can be moved anywhere on the neck, functioning as any of the twelve augmented chords. Is it really a different chord, or the same chord with a different name? What's your (Music) Theory?

Here's a simple little chord progression to help you get a feel for the sound that the Augmented chord creates. The progression follows the sequence I, I+, vi, IV, I, V, I. Most of the chords are combinations of two triads each. Then the Am chord is just a single triad with an open string in the bass. And the last C Major is a just a basic, simple C chord, which is actually a combination of all four triads from Pattern #3 (see pages 17 - 19). To help you see this, there are a couple of empty circles placed where missing notes *would* have been if they had not been cut off by the nut. Remember to always watch for and see the Cardinal Triads in each and every chord. Train your eyes, train your mind. Learn to look through the "Lens."

Because Augmented chords/triads are symmetrical, there is no way to invert the shape. This could be a Caug, Eaug., or Ab/G#aug., but here we'll just call it Caug. because that's where the tonal center is heard. Notice how it wants to pull you to the next chord.

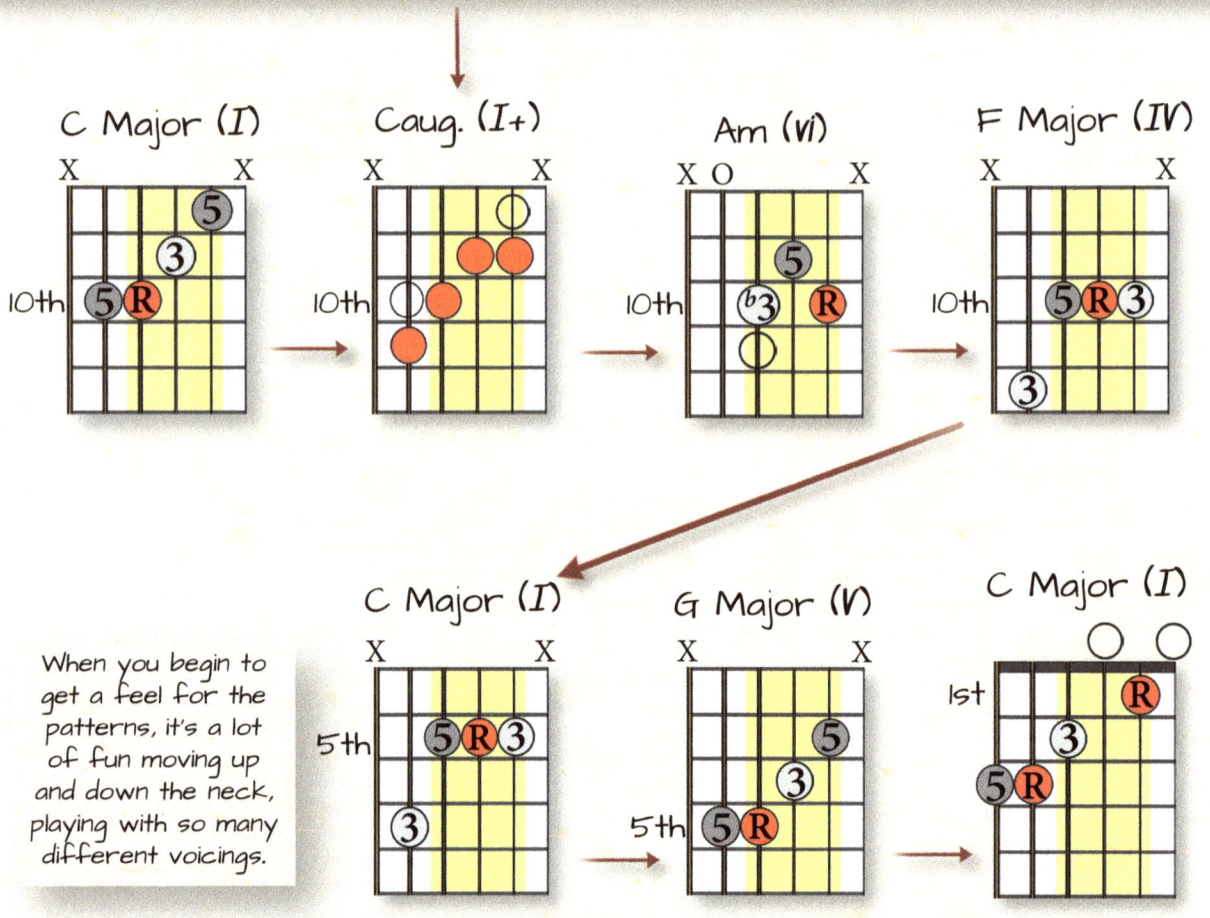

When you begin to get a feel for the patterns, it's a lot of fun moving up and down the neck, playing with so many different voicings.

"Music is not there to be understood, but to be. And the being of music is not in the notes, it is in the relationship between the notes, in the intervals, the pauses, the articulations, the silences."

—Pierre Boulez, 20th-century conductor

Diminished Triads

Now let's look at the Diminished shapes. Diminished triads/chords are similar to minor shapes, but the 5th note of the scale is *also* flattened. The formula is R - b3 - b5. Play the triads below. Listen closely to the sound, slip them into some of your chord progressions, and have fun getting used to the shapes.

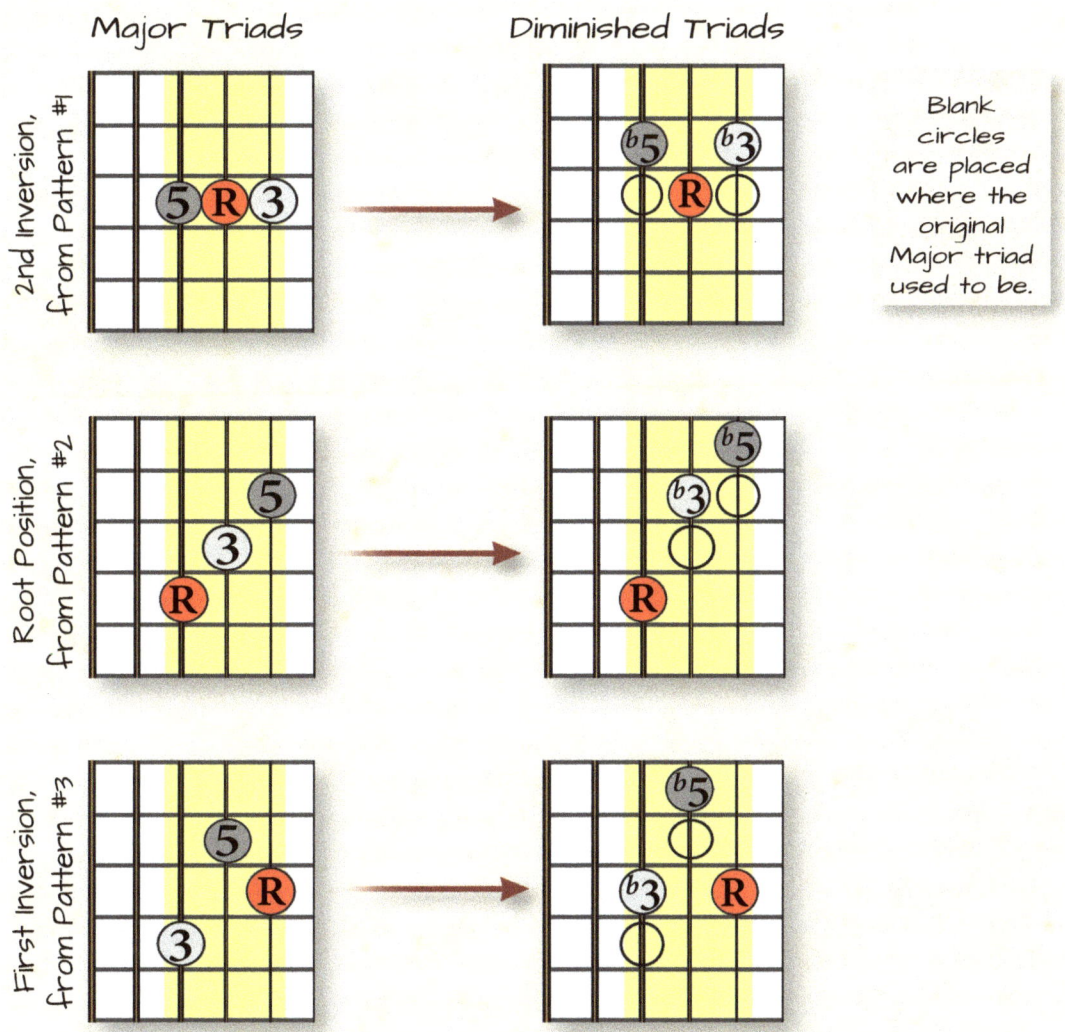

Blank circles are placed where the original Major triad used to be.

Diminished chords are usually used as transition chords, ascending or descending, from one chord to another. They have a beautiful, enchanting tension that wants to be resolved.

"... to forget yourself is to see everything else." — Jerry Garcia

Here's a fun little walk-down progression you can do using a Diminished chord. It begins on the 10th fret with a Major chord then walks down to a Diminished triad, then a dominant 7th and ends with the same A Major chord, but a uses a different inversion, lower on the neck (and a different voicing). Give it a try.

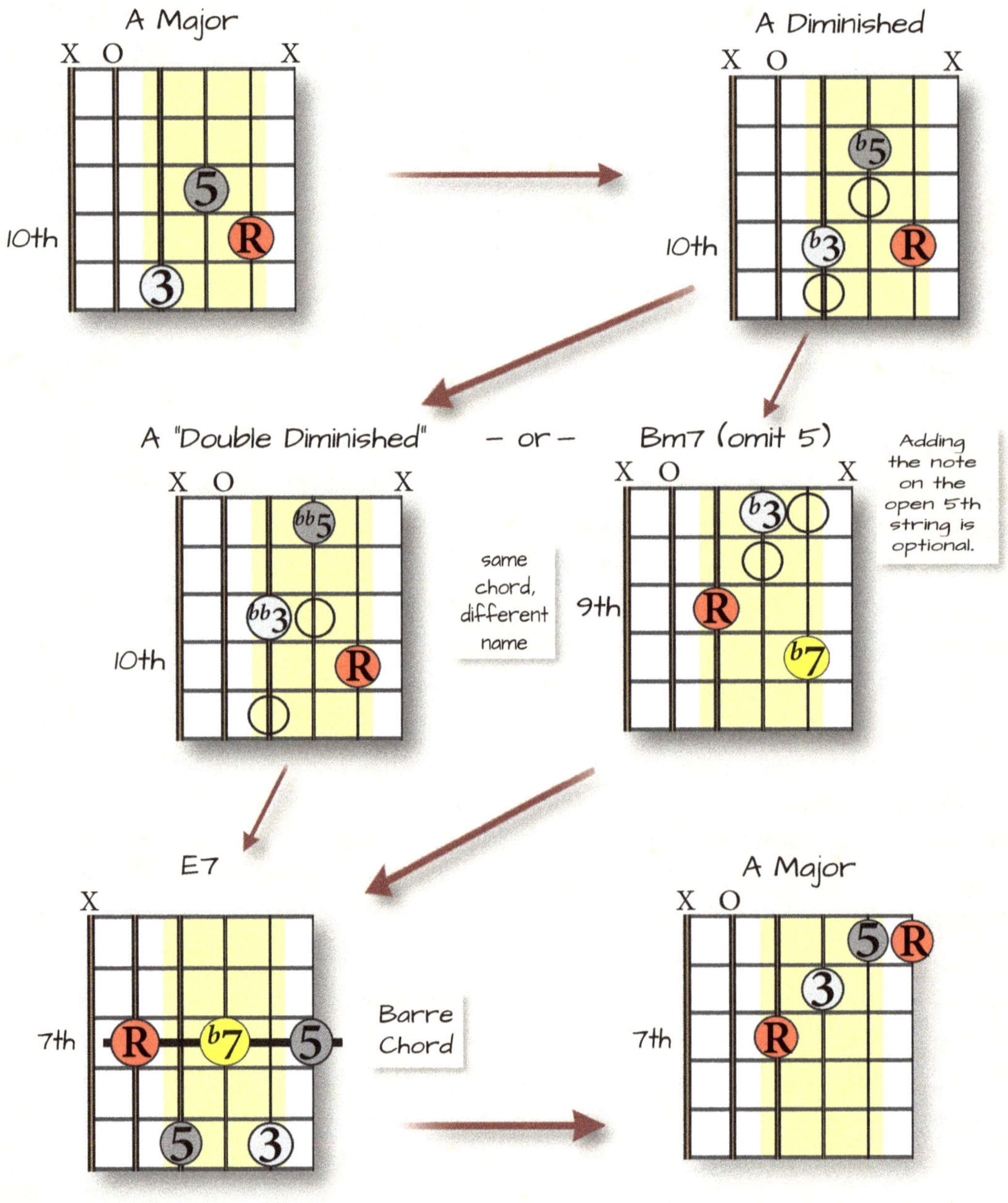

"If the doors of perception were cleansed, everything would appear to man as it is ~ infinite."
— Aldous Huxley, *The Doors of Perception*, 1954

The Diminished 7th Chord

Diminished chords can also be symmetrical, but only when a 7th is added. A fully diminished 7th chord is made of stacked minor third intervals, dividing the octave into four equal parts. Like augmented triads, any note can serve as the root, depending on the context in which the chord is used. In the diagram below, you can see how each square represents one of these chords and its position in the octave.

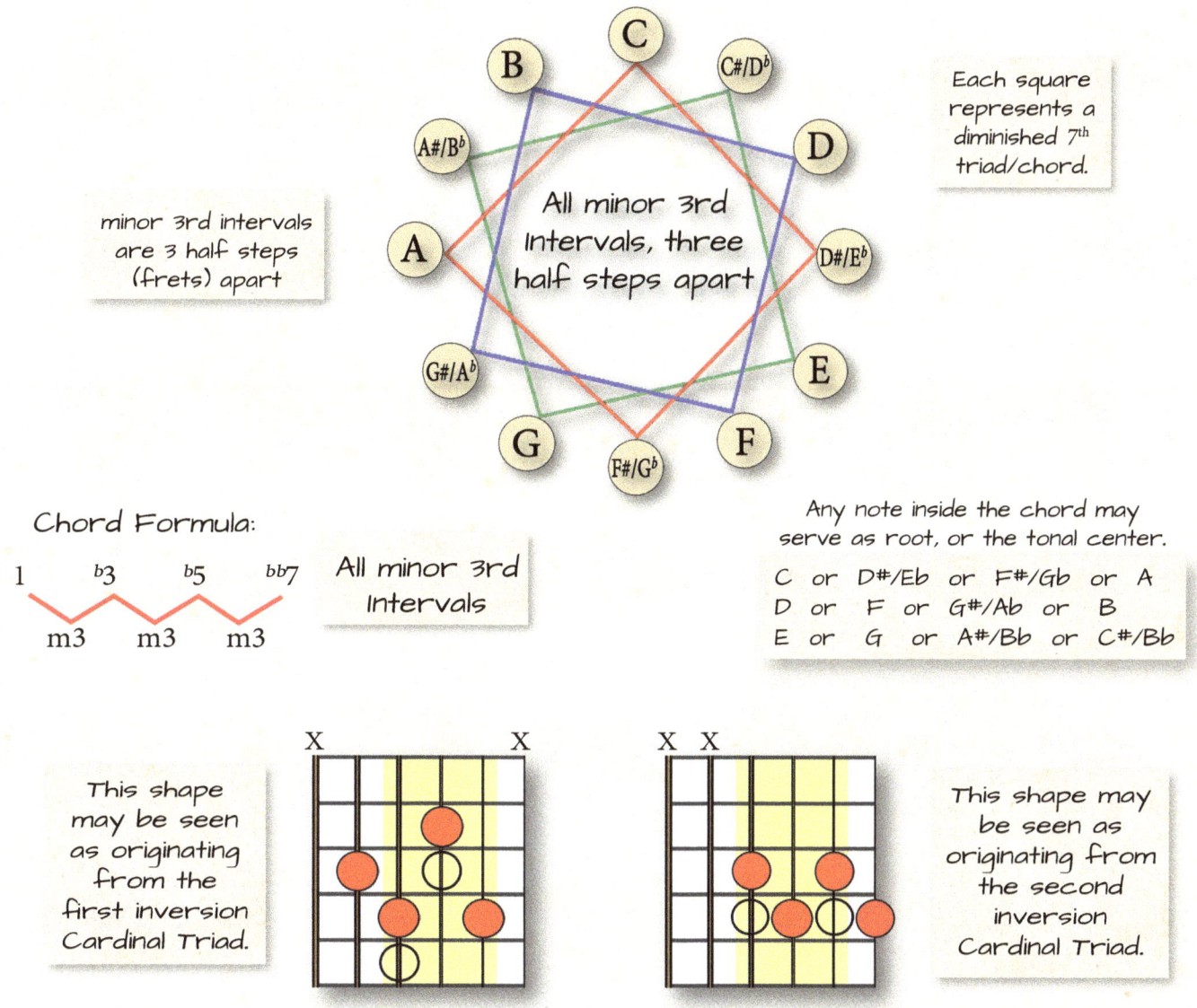

Each square represents a diminished 7th triad/chord.

minor 3rd intervals are 3 half steps (frets) apart

All minor 3rd Intervals, three half steps apart

Chord Formula:

1   b3   b5   bb7
  m3   m3   m3

All minor 3rd Intervals

Any note inside the chord may serve as root, or the tonal center.

C or D#/Eb or F#/Gb or A
D or F or G#/Ab or B
E or G or A#/Bb or C#/Bb

This shape may be seen as originating from the first inversion Cardinal Triad.

This shape may be seen as originating from the second inversion Cardinal Triad.

Two Diminished 7th Shapes, each on a different group of four strings. Notice that the 3rd and 5th notes of the Cardinal Triads have been flattened.

The diminished seventh chord is full of suspense, always pulling you toward something new and unexpected — like a hallway with four secret doors, each one acting as a leading tone into a different key. Its perfect symmetry makes it a masterful tool for modulation, pivoting effortlessly from one tonal center to another.

Dominant 7th Chords

The last group of chords we'll explore in this book are the dominant 7th chords. These chords carry a lot of tension that have a very strong "magnetic" pull back home to the tonic (the I chord).

7th chords usually contain four or more notes, which makes them full chords rather than triads. For our purposes, we'll focus first on the Cardinal Triads, adding the 7th note wherever it fits conveniently on the fretboard. We won't approach 7th chords with piano-style inversions; after all, we are *Guitarists*. ♥

The standard formula for a dominant 7th chord is R – 3 – 5 – ^{b}7. The ^{b}7 note can often be found either two frets below the root, or three frets above the 5th. Sometimes this can require omitting the root or the 5th so the chord fits comfortably under the fingers.

First, we'll find and focus on the Cardinal Triad in the illustration below, thinking about the best way to add the ^{b}7. On the following page, We will see some examples of how it all comes together.

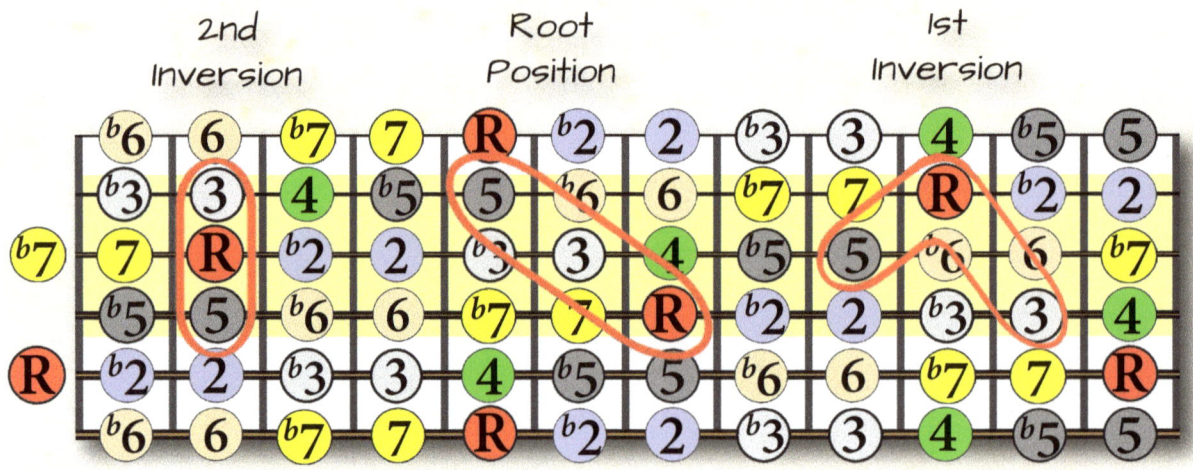

Art by Eric Montoya ~ Surrealist painter

🎵 Music 🎵
is the space between the notes.
— Claude Debussy

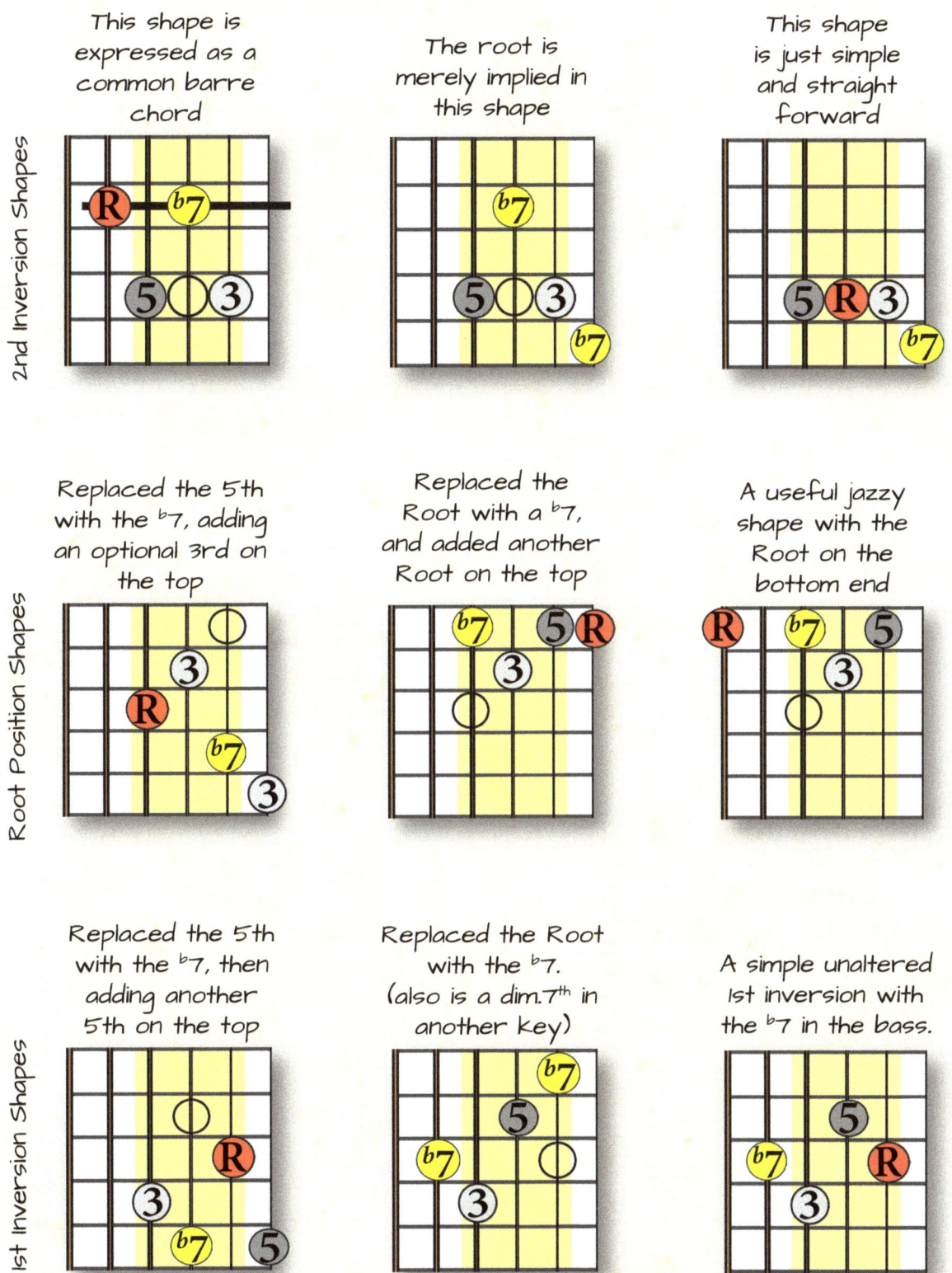

Remember, whenever you play a chord, *always* visualize the Cardinal Triad and its root note (use the empty circles to help you see them). See how it overlaps, intersects, or relates to the chord you are playing. Consistently train your mind to see the fretboard this way!

Basic Chord Formulas

Just a Few of My Favs
(for you to explore on your own)

Now that we have finished the lessons of this book, I thought you might like a short selection of chord formulas —chords for you to create by modifying and adding to the Cardinal Triads. Not a big list (and some of them we've already looked at a little bit), but it's a starting point for your own personal exploration. As you build these chords, visualize the location of the Cardinal Triad (as well as their expanded patterns) inside of the new chord shape. The chart below uses 'A' as the key and root note. So explore each chord in the key of A, with the different inversions and voicings along the neck.

Power Chord: 1 - 5
Major: 1 - 3 - 5
Minor: 1 - $\flat$3 - 5
Augmented: 1 - 3 - #5
Diminished: 1 - $\flat$3 - $\flat$5
Major 6: 1 - 3 - 5 - 6
minor 6: 1 - $\flat$3 - 5 - 6

Major 7th: 1 - 3 - 5 - 7
Dominant 7th: 1 - 3 - 5 - $\flat$7
minor 7th: 1 - $\flat$3 - 5 - $\flat$7
Augmented 7th: 1 - 3 - #5 - $\flat$7
Half Dim. 7th: 1 - $\flat$3 - $\flat$5 - $\flat$7
Diminished 7th: 1 - $\flat$3 - $\flat$5 - $\flat\flat$7
Tritone: 1 - 3 - $\flat$5 - 5

This is my little tritone formula. It's a lot of fun if you can figure out the right way to use it.

2 + 7 → 9
4 + 7 → 11
6 + 7 → 13

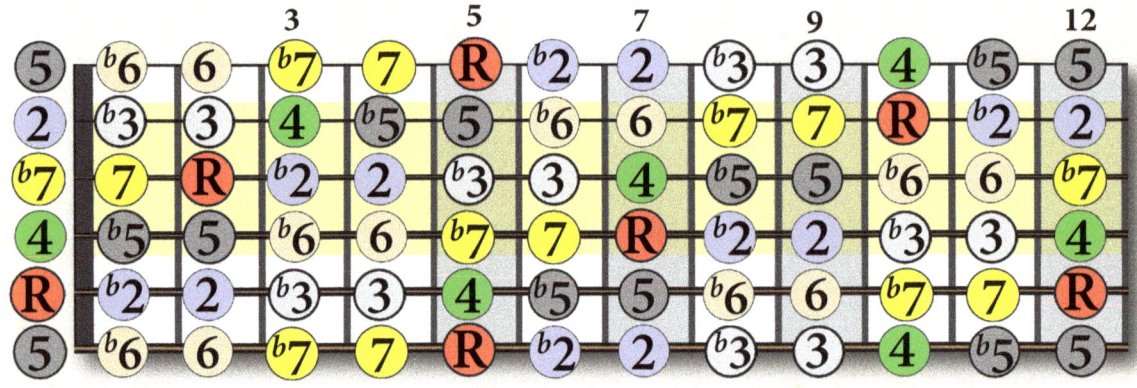

Diagram using "A" as the root of the scale.

Afterthoughts

Mastering the fretboard simply begins with a single seed: the visualization of the Cardinal Triads. Plant this seed in your mind's eye, let your understanding take root in these three shapes, and watch your command of the instrument branch out and blossom, transforming the entire fretboard into a map of clear, connected pathways.

Let these triads serve as more than chord shapes alone. **Use them as a nexus to weave together arpeggios, scales and melodies, into a seamless tapestry across the neck of the guitar!** Explore their patterns and voicings in every octave and corner of the fretboard. Discover the special qualities and abilities that each shape has to offer.

Be patient. It may take some time to fully absorb this material and integrate it into your own playing style, but have fun with it along the way. Eventually, the fretboard will feel like your own domain, and the music you create will blossom from the seed that we planted here.

This method reflects my own path and personal approach, one that has proven deeply rewarding for me. Your journey may lead you onto this path too —or it may lead you to an entirely different approach. If another path resonates more strongly, honor it fully. There may be other ways to the same horizon.

This book is not the final word on the fretboard. It's an entry point—a way into the living geometry of it, and a foundation upon which to build. Now the work continues. There will always be more to learn. Let your curiosity and passion guide you; never stop exploring!

"I say, follow your bliss and don't be afraid, and doors will open where you didn't know they were going to be. If you follow your bliss, doors will open for you that wouldn't have opened for anyone else."
— Joseph Campbell to Bill Moyers,
"The Power of Myth," Episode 1.

Blank Chord Charts

Blank Fretboard Charts

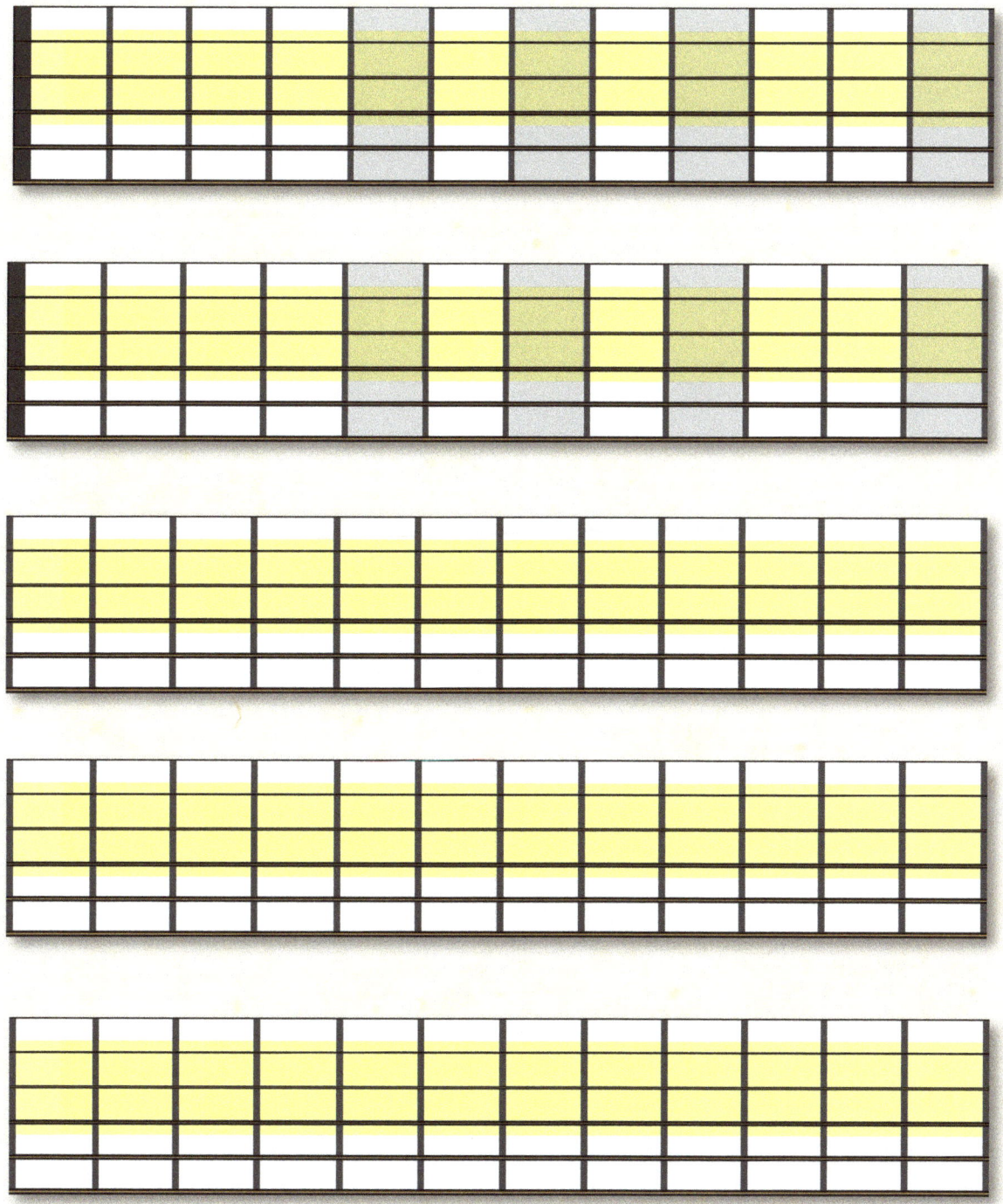

"There are things known and there are things unknown, and in between are the doors."
—Jim Morrison
Poet & Rock Singer

The Circle of Fifths
Learn it Well

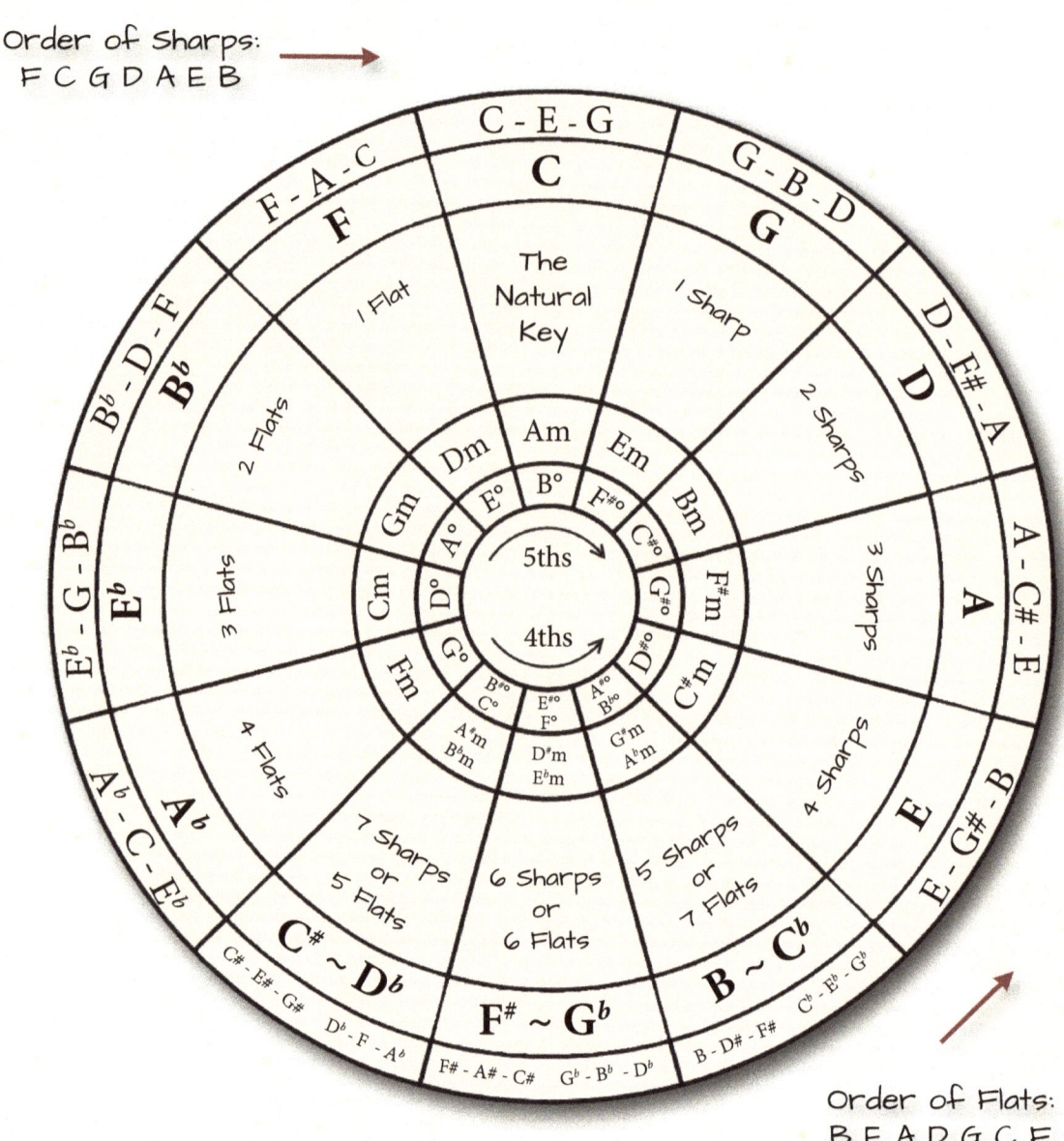

Order of Sharps: F C G D A E B

Order of Flats: B E A D G C F

```
F G A Bb C D E F
C D E F G A B C
G A B C D E F# G
D E F# G A B C# D
A B C# D E F# G# A
E F# G# A B C# D# E
B C# D# E F# G# A# B
```
Basic Scales Chart
(listed by order of sharps)

```
I  ii  iii  IV  V  vi  vii°
i  ii° III  iv  v  VI  VII
```
Top Row: Major Diatonic Chords
Bottom Row: minor Diatonic Chords

Glossary
(Terms that You Really Need to Know)

Alternative Tuning:
When an instrument is tuned differently from the standard. Alternative tunings can create unique voicings and textures that would be difficult or impossible to achieve otherwise. However, changing the tuning alters the patterns, shapes, and notes, making the fretboard feel like an entirely different instrument. In this way, the tuning becomes a fundamental part of the instrument's identity.

Arpeggio:
Playing the notes of a triad/chord individually, in succession.

Auxiliary Strings:
The 1st (E), 5th (A) and 6th (E) strings of the guitar. Strings that support and add to the other, more important strings (the most important strings are the 2nd, 3rd and 4th strings, on which the Cardinal Triads sit).

Cardinal Triads
A foundational set of three triad shapes from which all other chord forms and harmonic concepts are derived —through addition, alteration, and extension. They are not merely shapes, but organizing principles — the geometric axis of the fretboard. They serve as the Lens through which the entire neck is understood.
Positioned in the middle range of the strings, the Cardinal Triads fit naturally beneath the fingers, almost as if the human hand (and the guitar itself) were designed around them. By mastering the Cardinal Triads, a player begins to see the fretboard not as scattered notes, but as an organized system built from repeating patterns.

Circle of 5ths:
An organized way to look at the 12 notes/keys of the chromatic scale, where each successive note/key moves up by a 5th, moving clockwise around the circle. It is helpful for understanding the relationship between keys, the order of sharps/flats and other music theory concepts.

Chord:
Any three or more notes played simultaneously, in harmony together. Simple Major chords usually consist of a 1st (root), 3rd and 5th. The complexity of a chord grows as other notes are added (or subtracted). Power chords, lacking a third, fall outside this definition.

Chord Formula:
A list of notes (degrees of the scale) that are to be used for building a chord. The list is actually a pattern of intervals relative to the root. For example, 1 - 3 - 5 is the formula for a simple Major chord.

Chord Progression:

A pattern of chords used in a piece of music. The chord progressions are notated using Roman numerals. For example, a simple chord progression that uses the 1st, 4th and 5th chords of a key would be written as I - IV -V. So if we were playing in the key of E, that would make the chords E, A and B. The chords of a chord progression are the bones of a body of music. The melody is the flesh, and the rhythm is the life blood that pulses through it.

Chord Shape:

A particular finger placement on the fretboard that creates a chord in one area and another chord in a different area of the fretboard. Any given shape can be moved around the fretboard creating different chords wherever it is placed. It is best to see all triads and chords as shapes, or more importantly, as extensions and/or modifications of the Cardinal Triads. *Guitarists who memorize chords stay trapped. Those who see shapes move freely over the neck.*

Chromatic Scale:

A twelve-note scale that divides the octave into twelve equal pitches, from which all other scales are derived. It can be thought of as a kind of alphabet which forms chords and melodies into musical sentences.

Diatonic Scale:

A seven-note scale (eight, if you include the octave note), derived from the chromatic scale, created with a specific pattern of intervals or steps.

Dominant 7th vs. Major 7th:

A dominant 7th chord contains a flattened seventh, while a Major 7th chord contains a natural seventh. Though both are built on major triads, the dominant 7th creates tension and demands resolution, whereas the major 7th sounds stable and resolved.

Dyad:

Two notes played together, simultaneously. For example, a power chord may be a dyad.

Enharmonic Equivalent:

Notes, key signatures, or chords that have the same pitch but are named differently. For Example, an A# is the same pitch as an Bb. They are the same note, but named differently depending on the context in which they are used. We say that these are enharmonic equivalents.

Extended Chords:

An extended chord is a chord that includes notes beyond the basic triad, typically adding sevenths, ninths, elevenths, or thirteenths, etc.

Frequency:
The number of cycles or vibrations (a string moving back and forth) per second. Measured in Hertz (Hz).

Harmony:
Different pitches heard simultaneously, producing either consonant or dissonant sounds.

Half-Steps / Whole-Steps:
An octave is divided into twelve half steps (i.e. the chromatic scale), or six whole steps. Two half steps equal one whole step. On the guitar, each fret represents one half step.

Interval:
The distance between two notes (pitches), measured in half steps (semitones) or whole steps (tones).

Inversion:
Notation on the staff is inverted, and musical notes of a triad/chord are rotated into in a different order. The root is no longer in the bass (bottom of the staff). When chords/triads are inverted, alternative voicings are heard.

Major Chord:
Just a simple combination of the 1st, 3rd and 5th notes of the scale. Nothing is modified, added or subtracted. Purest, most natural and balanced sound.

Muse:
An awakener of hidden visions; one who perceives, interprets, and conveys the divine through artistic expression.

Natural Scale:
A musical scale with no accidentals (sharps or flats).

Octave:
The interval between two musical pitches where the higher pitch has exactly double the frequency of the lower one (a 2:1 ratio). This produces the most consonant sound in music, perceived as a "same-ness" of two notes (e.g., a high C and a low C). The octave can be divided into 12 equal semitones (the chromatic scale) but usually arranged into patterns of seven notes (diatonic scale). Ascending or descending to an octave feels like a return to origin, a completion of cycle, but on a higher/lower plane.

Relative Major/minor:
A pair of scales, chords, or keys that share the same key signature and the same set of notes, but have different tonal centers (e.g., Am and C Major).
Analogy: Like close relatives in a family, they share the same "DNA" (the set of notes), but have their own unique "personalities" (the tonal center and mood).

Root:
The foundational pitch upon which a chord or scale is built. In a scale, the root is the first and most important note, called the tonic. It is the "home" note and gives the scale its name (e.g., the note A is the root of the A Major scale). In a chord, the root is the note that gives the chord its letter name. It is the reference point for the chord's other notes (the third, fifth, etc.), even if it is not the lowest-sounding note in the voicing.

Symmetrical chord:
A symmetrical chord is built by stacking a single, repeating interval. The most common examples are the Augmented triad (two stacked Major thirds) and the Diminished seventh chord (three stacked minor thirds). Because the pattern divides the octave into equal parts, the chord is perfectly balanced. A key consequence of this symmetry is that any note in the chord can function as the root. This makes symmetrical chords ambiguous and incredibly useful for modulating smoothly to other keys.

Triad:
A chord consisting of exactly three notes: a root, a 3rd, and a 5th —built by stacking intervals of 3rds. There are four qualitative types of triads: Major, minor, diminished, and augmented. Extended chords (e.g., sevenths, ninths, etc.) are built by adding further 3rds on top of the triad. The triad is like the nucleus of the chord.
Also, triads are not only harmonic foundations but also melodic resources. Their notes can be arpeggiated into melodic patterns, woven into scale fragments, or voiced across octaves to create rhythmic and melodic ideas. The ability to see and use the three *Cardinal Triads* is one of the greatest assets a guitarist can have.

Tritone:
Traditionally defined as a musical interval composed of three whole steps or 6 half steps. It divides the octave exactly in half. It has a uniquely dissonant sound.

Voicing:
The specific arrangement, and octave placement of a triad/chord. The same chord played in different locations on the neck will mostly sound the same, but yet a little different, too. The key is the same, but the voicing has changed. Two different people may speak the same words, but their voices are different. Two musicians may play the same chord differently, each revealing a unique voicing.

Space for Notes

"The whole universe is made of sound. When we attune ourselves, we become instruments through which the harmony of the world is expressed."
— Hazrat Inayat Khan

Space for Notes

A432, where music meets nature's blueprint.

Space for Notes

www.ingramcontent.com/pod-product-compliance
Lightning Source LLC
Chambersburg PA
CBHW042359030426
42337CB00032B/5157